Careers in Focus

TECHNICIANS

THIRD EDITION

Ferguson
An imprint of Infobase Publishing

Ferguson
An imprint of Infobase Publishing
132 West 31st Street
New York NY 10001

Library of Congress Cataloging-in-Publication Data

Careers in focus. Technicians. — 3rd ed.
    p. cm.
  Includes index.
  ISBN-13: 978-0-8160-8021-2 (hardcover : alk. paper)
  ISBN-10: 0-8160-8021-6 (hardcover : alk. paper) 1. Industrial technicians—
Vocational guidance—Juvenile literature. I. Ferguson Publishing. II. Title:
Ferguson's Careers in focus.
  TA158.C365 2010
  602.3—dc22
                         2009047603

Ferguson books are available at special discounts when purchased in bulk quantities for businesses, associations, institutions, or sales promotions. Please call our
Special Sales Department in New York at (212) 967-8800 or (800) 322-8755.

You can find Ferguson on the World Wide Web at http://www.fergpubco.com

Text design by David Strelecky
Cover design by Takeshi Takahashi
Composition by Mary Susan Ryan-Flynn
Cover printed by Yurchak Printing, Landisville, Pa.
Book printed and bound by Yurchak Printing, Landisville, Pa.
Date printed: December 2011
Printed in the United States of America

This book is printed on acid-free paper.

All links and Web addresses were checked and verified to be correct at the time
of publication. Because of the dynamic nature of the Web, some addresses and
links may have changed since publication and may no longer be valid.

Table of Contents

Introduction

Technicians are specialists who work with scientists, engineers, and other professionals. They help these professionals in many activities, assist clients or customers, and supervise other skilled workers. Technicians work in many areas, such as factories, businesses, science labs, hospitals, and clinics. Some technicians are self-employed and work as consultants.

When looking at the range of job classifications in the traditional, hierarchical sense, the technician is the middleperson, falling between the scientist in the laboratory and the worker on the floor, between the engineer and the factory worker. The technician's realm lies where scientific thought meets practical application, where theory meets product. Little by little, however, industries and businesses are starting to work in new ways. All workers, be they scientists, managers, technicians, or line workers, are viewed as part of a team. Competencies and job knowledge are the new standards by which workers are valued, not rank alone. Thus many now see technician jobs as vital career paths in their own right, not simply junior scientists or engineers. Although the role of the technician is by nature supportive to their more prestigious or professional colleagues, those professionals could not do their work without the assistance of technicians. Would it make sense for an automotive engineer to spend hours fixing a car? Of course not. Assuming that the professional could even remember that far back in his or her training to perform the work, he or she does not know the technician's specialty as well as the technician. Thus the engineer concentrates on designing more efficient cars, and the technician makes it possible for people to keep driving them.

Society's growing reliance on technology has led to an increased need for technicians. As businesses switch to automated systems and as products become more technologically complex, technicians are needed to help design, implement, run, and repair systems or equipment, such as automobiles, airplanes, and computer networks. Even in nontechnical areas, there exists a certain expectation of speed, efficiency, and quality that is frequently the domain of the technician.

Technicians have also become increasingly appealing to businesses because of their overall cost compared to that of highly paid professionals such as engineers and scientists. While technicians in some industries work alongside professionals as valued members of the team, contributing their unique knowledge and skills in areas

I

professionals lack the time to develop fully, technicians in other industries are replacing professionals because they are less expensive to employ.

In a few areas technological advances are actually replacing technicians. Meteorological technicians, for example, are being phased out from jobs with the National Weather Service. Their painstaking instrument readings and weather data collection work can now be done entirely with high-tech instruments. Prepress technicians, EKG technicians, and home electronic entertainment equipment repairers are other technician specialties that are in decline because of advances in technology.

Overall, however, the future for technicians looks excellent, with opportunities for automobile service technicians, biomedical equipment technicians, environmental engineering technicians, environmental technicians, laser technicians, and surveying and mapping technicians predicted to be especially strong. As Louis Richman states in the article "The New Worker Elite" in *Fortune* magazine: "As the farm hand was to the agrarian economy of a century ago and the machine operator was to the electromechanical industrial era of recent decades, the technician is becoming the core employee of the digital Information Age."

Technician careers are appealing for another, very practical reason: They are good jobs that require a short educational path. Most technician careers initially require two years or less of postsecondary training. A few require a bachelor's degree to be competitive, and a very few do not require a high school diploma. For the aspiring engineer more interested in the day-to-day, practical applications of engineering rather than the theoretical side of science, a career as an engineering technician may be a perfect alternative to a career as an engineer. Technicians often work right alongside engineers and scientists, playing an important part in groundbreaking discoveries, long-awaited advances, and cutting-edge leaps. For a comparatively small investment in time and money, a person can emerge with a practical, highly marketable career.

The articles in *Careers in Focus: Technicians* appear in Ferguson's *Encyclopedia of Careers and Vocational Guidance,* but have been updated and revised with the latest information from the U.S. Department of Labor, professional organizations, and other sources.

The following paragraphs detail the sections and features that appear in the book.

The **Quick Facts** section provides a brief summary of the career, including recommended school subjects, personal skills, work environment, minimum educational requirements, salary ranges, certification or licensing requirements, and employment outlook. This section also provides acronyms and identification numbers for the following government classification indexes: the *Dictionary of Occupational Titles* (DOT), the *Guide for Occupational Exploration* (GOE), the National Occupational Classification (NOC) Index, and the Occupational Information Network (O*NET)-Standard Occupational Classification System (SOC) index. The DOT, GOE, and O*NET-SOC indexes have been created by the U.S. government; the NOC index is Canada's career classification system. Readers can use the identification numbers listed in the Quick Facts section to access further information about a career. Print editions of the DOT (*Dictionary of Occupational Titles*. Indianapolis, Ind.: JIST Works, 1991) and GOE (*Guide for Occupational Exploration*. Indianapolis, Ind.: JIST Works, 2001) are available at libraries. Electronic versions of the NOC (http://www23.hrdc-drhc.gc.ca) and O*NET-SOC (http://online.onetcenter.org) are available on the Internet. When no DOT, GOE, NOC, or O*NET-SOC numbers are present, this means that the U.S. Department of Labor or Human Resources Development Canada have not created a numerical designation for this career. In this instance, you will see the acronym "N/A," or not available.

The **Overview** section is a brief introductory description of the duties and responsibilities involved in this career. Oftentimes, a career may have a variety of job titles. When this is the case, alternative career titles are presented. Employment statistics are also provided, when available. The **History** section describes the history of the particular job as it relates to the overall development of its industry or field. **The Job** describes the primary and secondary duties of the job. **Requirements** discusses high school and postsecondary education and training requirements, any certification or licensing that is necessary, and other personal requirements for success in the job. **Exploring** offers suggestions on how to gain experience in or knowledge of the particular job before making a firm educational and financial commitment. The focus is on what can be done while still in high school (or in the early years of college) to gain a better understanding of the job. The **Employers** section gives an overview of typical places of employment for the job. **Starting Out** discusses the best ways to land that first job, be it through the college career services office, newspaper ads, Internet employment sites, or personal contact. The **Advancement** section describes what kind of career path to expect from the job and how to get there. **Earnings** lists salary ranges and describes the typical fringe benefits. The **Work Environment** section describes the typical surroundings and conditions of employment—whether indoors or outdoors, noisy or quiet, social or independent. Also discussed are typical hours worked, any seasonal fluctuations, and the stresses and strains of the job. The **Outlook** section summarizes the job in terms of the general economy and industry projections. For the most part, Outlook information is obtained from the U.S. Bureau of Labor Statistics and is supplemented by information gathered from professional associations. Job growth terms follow those used in the *Occupational Outlook Handbook*. Growth described as "much faster than the average" means an increase of 21 percent or more. Growth described as "faster than the average" means an increase of 14 to 20 percent. Growth described as "about as fast as the average" means an increase of 7 to 13 percent. Growth described as "more slowly than the average" means an increase of 3 to 6 percent. "Little or no change" means a decrease of 2 percent to an increase of 2 percent. "Decline" means a decrease of 3 percent or more. Each article ends with **For More Information,** which lists organizations that provide information on training, education, internships, scholarships, and job placement.

Careers in Focus: Technicians also includes photos, informative sidebars, and interviews with professionals in the field.

Agricultural Equipment Technicians

OVERVIEW

Agricultural equipment technicians work with modern farm machinery. They assemble, adjust, operate, maintain, modify, test, and even help design it. This machinery includes automatic animal feeding systems; milking machine systems; and tilling, planting, harvesting, irrigating, drying, and handling equipment. Agricultural equipment technicians work on farms or for agricultural machinery manufacturers or dealerships. They often supervise skilled mechanics and other workers who keep machines and systems operating at maximum efficiency. Approximately 31,000 agricultural equipment technicians are employed in the United States.

HISTORY

The history of farming equipment stretches back to prehistoric times, when the first agricultural workers developed the sickle. In the Middle Ages, the horse-drawn plow greatly increased farm production, and in the early 1700s, Jethro Tull designed and built the first mechanical seed planter, further increasing production. The industrial revolution brought advances in the design and use of specialized machinery for strenuous and repetitive work. It had a great impact on the agricultural industry, beginning in 1831 with Cyrus McCormick's invention of the reaper.

In the first half of the 20th century governmental experiment stations developed high-yield, standardized varieties of farm crops.

QUICK FACTS

School Subjects
Mathematics
Technical/shop

Personal Skills
Mechanical/manipulative
Technical/scientific

Work Environment
Indoors and outdoors
Primarily multiple locations

Minimum Education Level
Some postsecondary training

Salary Range
$21,380 to $31,860 to
$46,520

Certification or Licensing
None available

Outlook
About as fast as the average

DOT
624

GOE
03.03.01, 05.03.01

NOC
7316

O*NET-SOC
45-2091.00, 49-3041.00

This, combined with the establishment of agricultural equipment-producing companies, caused a boom in the production of farm machinery. In the late 1930s an abundance of inexpensive petroleum spurred the development of gasoline- and diesel-run farm machinery. During the early 1940s the resulting explosion in complex and powerful farm machinery multiplied production and replaced most of the horses and mules used on farms in the United States.

Modern farming is heavily dependent on very complex and expensive machinery. Highly trained and skilled technicians and farm mechanics are therefore required to install, operate, maintain, and modify this machinery, thereby ensuring the nation's farm productivity. Recent developments in agricultural mechanization and automation make the career of agricultural equipment technicians both challenging and rewarding. Sophisticated machines are being used to plant, cultivate, harvest, and process food; to contour, drain, and renovate land; and to clear land and harvest forest products in the process. Qualified agricultural equipment technicians are needed not only to service and sell this equipment, but also to manage it on the farm.

Farming has become a highly competitive, big business. A successful farmer may have thousands or even millions of dollars invested in land and machinery. For this investment to pay off, it is vital to keep the machinery in excellent operating condition. Prompt and reliable service from the farm equipment manufacturer and dealer is necessary for the success of both farmer and dealer. Interruptions or delays because of poor service are costly for everyone involved. To provide good service, manufacturers and dealers need technicians and specialists who possess agricultural and engineering knowledge in addition to technical skills.

THE JOB

Agricultural equipment technicians work in a wide variety of jobs both on and off the farm. In general, most agricultural equipment technicians find employment in one of three areas: equipment manufacturing, equipment sales and service, and on-farm equipment management.

Equipment manufacturing technicians are involved primarily with the design and testing of agricultural equipment such as farm machinery; irrigation, power, and electrification systems; soil and water conservation equipment; and agricultural harvesting and processing equipment. There are two kinds of technicians working in this field: agricultural engineering technicians and agricultural equipment test technicians.

Agricultural engineering technicians work under the supervision of design engineers. They prepare original layouts and complete detailed drawings of agricultural equipment. They also review plans, diagrams, and blueprints to ensure that new products comply with company standards and design specifications. In order to do this they must use their knowledge of biological, engineering, and design principles. They also must keep current on all of the new equipment and materials being developed for the industry to make sure the machines run at their highest capacity.

Agricultural equipment test technicians test and evaluate the performance of agricultural machinery and equipment. In particular, they make sure the equipment conforms with operating requirements, such as horsepower, resistance to vibration, and strength and hardness of parts. They test equipment under actual field conditions on company-operated research farms and under more controlled conditions. They work with test equipment and recording instruments such as bend-fatigue machines, dynamometers, strength testers, hardness meters, analytical balances, and electronic recorders.

Test technicians are also trained in methods of recording the data gathered during these tests. Using algebraic formulas they compute values such as horsepower and tensile strength; they report their findings using graphs, tables, and sketches.

After the design and testing phases are complete, other agricultural equipment technicians work with engineers to perform any necessary adjustments in the equipment design. By performing these functions under the general supervision of the design engineer, technicians do the engineers' "detective work" so the engineers can devote more time to research and development.

Large agricultural machinery companies may employ agricultural equipment technicians to supervise production, assembly, and plant operations.

Most manufacturers market their products through regional sales organizations to individual dealers. Technicians may serve as *sales representatives* of regional sales offices, where they are assigned a number of dealers in a given territory and sell agricultural equipment directly to them. They may also conduct sales-training programs for the dealers to help them become more effective salespeople.

These technicians are also qualified to work in sales positions within dealerships, either as *equipment sales workers* or *parts clerks*. They are required to perform equipment demonstrations for customers. They also appraise the value of used equipment for trade-in allowances. Technicians in these positions may advance to sales or parts manager positions.

Some technicians involved in sales become *systems specialists*, who work for equipment dealerships, assisting farmers in the planning and installation of various kinds of mechanized systems, such as irrigation or materials-handling systems, grain bins, or drying systems.

In the service area, technicians may work as *field service representatives*, forming a liaison between the companies they represent and the dealers. They assist the dealers in product warranty work, diagnose service problems, and give seminars or workshops on new service information and techniques. These types of service technicians may begin their careers as specialists in certain kinds of repairs. *Hydraulic specialists*, for instance, maintain and repair the component parts of hydraulic systems in tractors and other agricultural machines. *Diesel specialists* rebuild, calibrate, and test diesel pumps, injectors, and other diesel engine components.

Many service technicians work as service managers or parts department managers. *Service managers* assign duties to the repair workers, diagnose machinery problems, estimate repair costs for customers, and manage the repair shop.

Parts department managers in equipment dealerships maintain inventories of all the parts that may be requested either by customers or by the service departments of the dealership. They deal directly with customers, parts suppliers, and dealership managers and must have good sales and purchasing skills. They also must be effective business managers.

Technicians working on the farm have various responsibilities, the most important of which is keeping machinery in top working condition during the growing season. During off-season periods they may overhaul or modify equipment or simply keep the machinery in good working order for the next season.

Some technicians find employment as *on-farm machinery managers*, usually working on large farms servicing or supervising the servicing of all automated equipment. They also monitor the field operation of all machines and keep complete records of costs, utilization, and repair procedures relating to the maintenance of each piece of mechanical equipment.

REQUIREMENTS

High School

To prepare for this career you should take as many mathematics, technical/shop, and mechanical drawing classes as you can. Take science classes, including courses in earth science, to gain some insight into agriculture, soil conservation, and the environment. Look into adult education programs available to high school students; in such a program, you may be able to enroll in pre-engineering courses.

Postsecondary Training
A high school diploma is necessary to enter this field, and some college and specialized experience is also important. A four-year education, along with some continuing education courses, can be very helpful in pursuing work, particularly if you're seeking jobs with the government.

Postsecondary education for the agricultural equipment technician should include courses in general agriculture, agricultural power and equipment, practical engineering, hydraulics, agricultural-equipment business methods, electrical equipment, engineering, social science, economics, and sales techniques. On-the-job experience during the summer is invaluable and frequently is included as part of the regular curriculum in these programs. Students are placed on farms, functioning as technicians-in-training. They also may work in farm equipment dealerships where their time is divided between the sales, parts, and service departments. Occupational experience, one of the most important phases of the postsecondary training program, gives students an opportunity to discover which field best suits them and which phase of the business they prefer. Upon completion of this program, most technical and community colleges award an associate's degree.

Other Requirements
The work of the agricultural equipment technician is similar to that of an engineer. You must have a knowledge of physical science and engineering principles and enough mathematical background to work with these principles. You must have a working knowledge of farm crops, machinery, and all agricultural-related products. You should be detail-oriented. You should also have people skills, as you'll be working closely with professionals, other technicians, and farmers.

EXPLORING

If you live in a farming community, you've probably already had some experience with farming equipment. Vocational agriculture education programs in high schools can be found in most rural settings, many suburban settings, and even in some urban schools. The teaching staff and counselors in these schools can provide considerable information about this career.

Light industrial machinery is now used in almost every industry. It is always helpful to watch machinery being used and to talk with people who own, operate, and repair it.

Summer and part-time work on a farm, in an agricultural equipment manufacturing plant, or in an equipment sales and service business offers opportunities to work on or near agricultural and light industrial machinery. Such a job may provide you with a clearer idea about the various activities, challenges, rewards, and possible limitations of this career.

EMPLOYERS

Approximately 31,000 agricultural equipment technicians are employed in the United States. Depending on their area of specialization, technicians work for engineers, manufacturers, scientists, sales and services companies, and farmers. They can also find work with government agencies, such as the U.S. Department of Agriculture.

STARTING OUT

It is still possible to enter this career by starting as an inexperienced worker in a machinery manufacturing plant or on a farm, learning machine technician skills on the job. However, this approach is becoming increasingly difficult due to the complexity of modern machinery. Because of this, some formal classroom training is usually necessary, and many people find it difficult to complete even part-time study of the field's theory and science while also working a full-time job.

Operators and managers of large, well-equipped farms and farm equipment companies in need of employees keep in touch with colleges offering agricultural equipment programs. Students who do well during their occupational experience period usually have an excellent chance of going to work for the same employer after graduation. Many colleges have an interview day on which personnel representatives of manufacturers, distributors, farm owners or managers, and dealers are invited to recruit students completing technician programs. In general, any student who does well in a training program can expect employment immediately upon graduation.

ADVANCEMENT

Opportunities for advancement and self-employment are excellent for those with the initiative to keep abreast of continuing developments in the farm equipment field. Technicians often attend company schools in sales and service or take advanced evening courses in colleges.

EARNINGS

Agricultural technicians working for the government may be able to enter a position at GS-5 (government wage scale), which was $27,026 in 2009. The U.S. Department of Labor reports that median annual earnings for agricultural equipment mechanics were $31,860 in 2008. Hourly wages ranged from less than $10.28 ($26,080 a year) to more than $22.37 ($46,520 a year). Those working on farms often receive room and board as a supplement to their annual salary. The salary that technicians eventually receive depends—as do most salaries—on individual ability, initiative, and the supply of skilled technicians in the field of work or locality. There is opportunity to work overtime during planting and harvesting seasons.

In addition to their salaries, most technicians receive fringe benefits such as health and retirement packages, paid vacations, and other benefits similar to those received by engineering technicians. Technicians employed in sales are usually paid a commission in addition to their base salary.

WORK ENVIRONMENT

Working conditions vary according to the type of field chosen. Technicians who are employed by large farming operations will work indoors or outdoors depending on the season and the tasks that need to be done. Planning machine overhauls and the directing of such work usually are done in enclosed spaces equipped for that purpose. As implied by its name, field servicing and repairs are done in the field.

Some agricultural equipment sales representatives work in their own or nearby communities, while others must travel extensively.

Technicians in agricultural equipment research, development, and production usually work under typical factory conditions: some work in an office or laboratory; others work in a manufacturing plant; or, in some cases, field testing and demonstration are performed where the machinery will be used.

For technicians who assemble, adjust, modify, or test equipment and for those who provide customer service, application studies, and maintenance services, the surroundings may be similar to large automobile service centers.

In all cases, safety precautions must be a constant concern. Appropriate clothing, an acute awareness of one's environment, and careful lifting or hoisting of heavy machinery must be standard. While safety practices have improved greatly over the years, certain risks do exist. Heavy lifting may cause injury, and burns and cuts are always possible. The surroundings may be noisy and grimy. Some work is performed in cramped or awkward physical positions. Gasoline fumes and odors from oil products are a constant factor. Most technicians ordinarily work a 40-hour week, but emergency repairs may require overtime.

OUTLOOK

Employment of agricultural equipment technicians is expected to experience growth about as fast as the average through 2018, according to the *Occupational Outlook Handbook*. However, agricultural equipment businesses now demand more expertise than ever before. A variety of complex specialized machines and mechanical devices are steadily being produced and modified to help farmers improve the quality and productivity of their labor. These machines require trained technicians to design, produce, test, sell, and service them. Trained workers also are needed to instruct the final owners in their proper repair, operation, and maintenance.

In addition, the agricultural industry is adopting advanced computer, hydraulics, and electronic technology. Computer skills are becoming more and more useful in this field. Precision farming will also require specialized training as more agricultural equipment is linked to satellite systems.

As agriculture becomes more technical, the agricultural equipment technician will assume an increasingly vital role in helping farmers solve problems that interfere with efficient production. These opportunities exist not only in the United States, but also worldwide. As agricultural economies everywhere become mechanized, inventive technicians with training in modern business principles will find expanding employment opportunities abroad.

FOR MORE INFORMATION

To read equipment sales statistics, agricultural reports, and other news of interest to agricultural equipment technicians, visit

Association of Equipment Manufacturers
6737 West Washington Street, Suite 2400
Milwaukee, WI 53214-5647
Tel: 414-272-0943

Email: info@aem.org
http://www.aem.org

Visit the following Web site to learn about publications and read industry news:
Farm Equipment Manufacturers Association
1000 Executive Parkway, Suite 100
St. Louis, MO 63141-6369
Tel: 314-878-2304
Email: info@farmequip.org
http://www.farmequip.org

For information on student chapters and the many activities it offers, contact
National FFA Organization
6060 FFA Drive
PO Box 68960
Indianapolis, IN 46268-0960
Tel: 317-802-6060
Email: membership@ffa.org
http://www.ffa.org

Automobile Service Technicians

OVERVIEW

Automobile service technicians maintain and repair cars, vans, small trucks, and other vehicles. Using both hand tools and specialized diagnostic test equipment, they pinpoint problems and make the necessary repairs or adjustments. In addition to performing complex and difficult repairs, technicians perform a number of routine maintenance procedures, such as oil changes, tire rotation, and battery replacement. Technicians interact frequently with customers to explain repair procedures and discuss maintenance needs. Approximately 763,000 automotive service technicians work in the United States.

HISTORY

By the mid-1920s, the automobile industry began to change America. As automobiles changed through the years, mechanics—or automobile service technicians, as they are now called—have kept them running. The "Big Three" automobile makers—Ford, General Motors, and Chrysler—produced millions of cars for a public eager for the freedom and mobility the automobile promised. With the ill-prepared roads suddenly overrun by inexperienced drivers, accidents and breakdowns became common. People not only were unskilled in driving but also were ignorant of the basic maintenance and service the automobile required. It suddenly became apparent that a new profession was in the making.

In 1899 the American Motor Company opened a garage in New York and advertised "competent mechanics always on hand to make

14

repairs when necessary." Gradually, other repair "garages" opened in larger cities, but they were few and far between. Automobiles were much simpler in the early years. Basic maintenance and minor repairs often could be performed by the owner or someone with general mechanical aptitude.

As cars became more complex, the need for qualified technicians grew. Dealerships began to hire mechanics to handle increasing customer concerns and complaints. Gas stations also began to offer repair and maintenance services. The profession of automobile mechanic was suddenly in big demand.

By the 1950s automobile service and repair garages were common throughout the United States, in urban and rural areas alike. Most mechanics learned the trade through hands-on experience as an apprentice or on their own through trial and error. When automakers began packing their cars with new technology, involving complex electrical circuitry, and computer-controlled mechanisms as well as basic design changes, it became apparent that mechanics would need comprehensive training to learn new service and repair procedures. Until the 1970s, there was no standard by which automobile service technicians were trained. In 1972 the National Institute for Automotive Service Excellence (ASE) was established. It set national training standards for new technicians and provided continuing education and certification for existing technicians when new technology became widespread in the field.

Today, the demand for trained, highly skilled professionals in the service industry is more important than ever. To keep up with the technology that is continually incorporated in new vehicles, service technicians require more intensive training than in the past. Today, mechanics who have completed a high level of formal training are generally called automobile service technicians. They have studied the complexities of the latest automotive technology, from computerized mechanisms in the engine to specialized diagnostic testing equipment.

THE JOB

Many automobile service technicians feel that the most exciting part of their work is troubleshooting—locating the source of a problem and successfully fixing it. Diagnosing mechanical, electrical, and computer-related troubles requires a broad knowledge of how cars work, the ability to make accurate observations, and the patience to logically determine what went wrong. Technicians agree that it frequently is more difficult to find the problem than it is to fix it. With experience, knowing where to look for problems becomes second nature.

Generally, there are two types of automobile service technicians: *generalists* and *specialists*. Generalists work under a broad umbrella of repair and service duties. They have proficiency in several kinds of light repairs and maintenance of many different types of automobiles. Their work, for the most part, is routine and basic. Specialists concentrate in one or two areas and learn to master them for many different car makes and models. Today, in light of the sophisticated technology common in new cars, there is an increasing demand for specialists. Automotive systems are not as easy or as standard as they used to be, and they now require many hours of experience to master. To gain a broad knowledge in auto maintenance and repair, specialists usually begin as generalists.

When a car does not operate properly, the owner brings it to a service technician and describes the problem. At a dealership or larger shop, the customer may talk with a *repair service estimator,* who writes down the customer's description of the problem and relays it to the service technician. The technician may test-drive the car or use diagnostic equipment, such as motor analyzers, spark plug testers, or compression gauges, to determine the problem. If a customer explains that the car's automatic transmission does not shift gears at the right times, the technician must know how the functioning of the transmission depends on the engine vacuum, the throttle pressure, and—more common in newer cars—the onboard computer. Each factor must be thoroughly checked. With each test, clues help the technician pinpoint the cause of the malfunction. After successfully diagnosing the problem, the technician makes the necessary adjustments or repairs. If a part is too badly damaged or worn to be repaired, he or she replaces it after first consulting the car owner, explaining the problem, and estimating the cost.

Normal use of an automobile inevitably causes wear and deterioration of parts. Generalist automobile technicians handle many of the routine maintenance tasks to help keep a car in optimal operating condition. They change oil, lubricate parts, and adjust or replace components of any of the car's systems that might cause a malfunction, including belts, hoses, spark plugs, brakes, filters, and transmission and coolant fluids.

Technicians who specialize in the service of specific parts usually work in large shops with multiple departments, car diagnostic centers, franchised auto service shops, or small independent shops that concentrate on a particular type of repair work.

Tune-up technicians evaluate and correct engine performance and fuel economy. They use diagnostic equipment and other computerized devices to locate malfunctions in fuel, ignition, and emissions-control systems. They adjust ignition timing and valves and may replace spark plugs, points, triggering assemblies in electronic ignitions, and other components to ensure maximum engine efficiency.

Electrical-systems technicians have been in healthy demand in recent years. They service and repair the complex electrical and computer circuitry common in today's automobile. They use both sophisticated diagnostic equipment and simpler devices such as ammeters, ohmmeters, and voltmeters to locate system malfunctions. In addition to having excellent electrical skills, electrical-systems technicians require basic mechanical aptitude to get at electrical and computer circuitry located throughout the automobile.

Front-end technicians are concerned with suspension and steering systems. They inspect, repair, and replace front-end parts such as springs, shock absorbers, and linkage parts such as tie rods and ball joints. They also align and balance wheels.

Brake repairers work on drum and disk braking systems, parking brakes, and hydraulic systems. They inspect, adjust, remove, repair, and reinstall such items as brake shoes, disk pads, drums, rotors, wheel and master cylinders, and hydraulic fluid lines. Some specialize in both brake and front-end work.

Transmission technicians adjust, repair, and maintain gear trains, couplings, hydraulic pumps, valve bodies, clutch assemblies, and other parts of automatic transmission systems. Transmissions have become complex and highly sophisticated mechanisms in newer model automobiles. Technicians require special training to learn how they function.

An automobile service technician repairs an engine. *(Stanley Walker, Syracuse Newspapers/The Image Works)*

Automobile-radiator mechanics clean radiators using caustic solutions. They locate and solder leaks and install new radiator cores. In addition, some radiator mechanics repair car heaters and air conditioners and solder leaks in gas tanks.

Alternative fuel technicians are relatively new additions to the field. This specialty has evolved with the nation's efforts to reduce its dependence on foreign oil by exploring alternative fuels, such as ethanol, biobutanol, and electricity.

As more automobiles rely on a variety of electronic components, technicians have become more proficient in the basics of electronics, even if they are not electronics specialists. Electronic controls and instruments are located in nearly all the systems of today's cars. Many previously mechanical functions in automobiles are being replaced by electronics, significantly altering the way repairs are performed. Diagnosing and correcting problems with electronic components often involves the use of specialty tools and computers.

Automobile service technicians use an array of tools in their everyday work, ranging from simple hand tools to computerized diagnostic equipment. Technicians supply their own hand tools at an investment of $6,000 to $25,000 or more, depending on their specialty. It is usually the employer's responsibility to furnish the larger power tools, engine analyzers, and other test equipment.

To maintain and increase their skills and to keep up with new technology, automobile technicians must regularly read service and repair manuals, shop bulletins, and other publications. They must also be willing to take part in training programs given by manufacturers or at vocational schools. Those who have voluntary certification must periodically retake exams to keep their credentials.

REQUIREMENTS
High School
In today's competitive job market, aspiring automobile service technicians need a high school diploma to land a job that offers growth possibilities, a good salary, and challenges. There is a big demand in the automotive service industry to fill entry-level positions with well-trained, highly skilled persons. Technology demands more from the technician than it did 10 years ago.

In high school, you should take automotive and shop classes, mathematics, English, and computer classes. Adjustments and repairs to many car components require the technician to make numerous computations, for which good mathematical skills are essential. Good reading skills are also valuable, as a technician must do a lot of reading to stay competitive in today's job market. English classes will prepare you to handle the many volumes of repair manuals and trade journals you will need to remain informed. Computer skills are also vital, as computers are now common in most repair shops. They keep track of customers' histories and parts and often detail repair procedures. Use of computers in repair shops will only increase in the future.

Postsecondary Training

Employers today prefer to hire only those who have completed some kind of formal training program in automobile mechanics—usually a minimum of two years. A wide variety of such programs are offered at community colleges, vocational schools, independent organizations, and manufacturers. Many community colleges and vocational schools around the country offer postsecondary programs accredited by the National Automotive Technicians Education Foundation and the Accrediting Commission of Career Schools and Colleges of Technology. Postsecondary training programs prepare students through a blend of classroom instruction and hands-on practical experience. They range in length from six months to two years or more, depending on the type of program. Shorter programs usually involve intensive study. Longer programs typically alternate classroom courses with periods of work experience. Some two-year programs include courses on applied mathematics, reading and writing skills, and business practices and lead to an associate's degree.

Some programs are conducted in association with automobile manufacturers. Students combine work experience with hands-on classroom study of up-to-date equipment and new cars provided by manufacturers. In other programs, students alternate time in the classroom with internships in dealerships or service departments. These students may take up to four years to finish their training, but they become familiar with the latest technology and also earn a modest salary.

Certification or Licensing

Automobile service technicians may be certified by the ASE in one of the following eight areas: automatic transmission/transaxle, brakes, electrical/electronic systems, engine performance, engine repair, heating and air conditioning, manual drive train and axles, and suspension and steering. Those who become certified in all eight areas are known as master mechanics. Although certification is voluntary, it is a widely recognized standard of achievement for automobile technicians and is highly valued by many employers. Certification also provides the means and opportunity to advance. To maintain their certification, technicians must retake the examination for their specialties every five years. Many employers only hire ASE-accredited technicians and base salaries on the level of the technicians' accreditation. There are other specialized certifications available, including one for technicians who repair compressed natural gas vehicles.

Other Requirements

To be a successful automobile service technician, you must be patient and thorough in your work; a shoddy repair job may put the driver's life at risk. You must have excellent troubleshooting skills and be able to logically deduce the cause of system malfunctions.

EXPLORING

Many community centers offer general auto maintenance and mechanics workshops where you can practice working on real cars and learn from instructors. Trade magazines are excellent sources for learning what's new in the industry and can be found at most public libraries or large bookstores. Many public television stations broadcast automobile maintenance and repair programs that can help beginners learn about various types of cars.

Working on cars as a hobby provides valuable firsthand experience in the work of a technician. An after-school or weekend part-time job in a repair shop or dealership can give you a feel for the general atmosphere and kinds of problems technicians face on the job. Oil and tire changes, battery and belt replacement, and even pumping gas may be some of the things you will be asked to do on the job; this work will give you valuable experience before you move on to more complex repairs. Experience with vehicle repair work in the armed forces is another way to pursue your interest in this field.

EMPLOYERS

Approximately 763,000 automotive service technicians are employed in the United States. Because the automotive industry is so vast, automobile service technicians have many choices concerning type of shop and geographic location in which to work. Automobile repairs are needed all over the country, in large cities as well as rural areas.

The majority of automobile service technicians work for automotive dealers and independent automotive repair shops and gasoline service stations. The field offers a variety of other employment options as well. The U.S. Department of Labor estimates that nearly 16 percent of automobile service technicians are self-employed. Other employers include franchises such as Pep Boys and Midas that offer routine repairs and maintenance, and automotive service departments of automotive and home supply stores. Some automobile service technicians maintain fleets for taxicab and automobile leasing companies or for government agencies with large automobile fleets.

Technicians with experience and/or ASE certification certainly have more career choices. Some master mechanics may go on to teach at technical and vocational schools or at community colleges. Others put in many years working for someone else and go into business for themselves after they have gained the experience to handle many types of repairs and oversee other technicians.

STARTING OUT

The best way to start out in this field is to attend one of the many postsecondary training programs available throughout the country. Trade and technical schools usually provide job placement assistance for their graduates. Schools often have contacts with local employers who need to hire well-trained people. Frequently, employers post job openings at nearby trade schools with accredited programs. Job openings are frequently listed on the Internet through regional and national automotive associations or career networks.

A decreasing number of technicians learn the trade on the job as apprentices. Their training consists of working for several years under the guidance of experienced mechanics. Fewer employers today are willing to hire apprentices due to the time and money it takes to train them. Those who do learn their skills on the job will inevitably require some formal training if they wish to advance and stay in step with the changing industry.

Intern programs sponsored by car manufacturers or independent organizations provide students with excellent opportunities to actually work with prospective employers. Internships can provide students with valuable contacts who will be able to recommend future employers once they have completed their training. Many students may even be hired by the shop at which they interned.

ADVANCEMENT

With today's complex automobile components requiring hundreds of hours of study and practice to master, more repair shops prefer to hire specialists. Generalist automobile technicians advance as they gain experience and become specialists. Other technicians advance to diesel repair, where the pay may be higher. Those with good communication and planning skills may advance to shop foreman or service manager at large repair shops or to sales workers at dealerships. Master mechanics with good business skills often go into business for themselves and open their own shops.

EARNINGS

Salary ranges of automobile service technicians vary depending on the level of experience, type of shop the technician works in, and geographic location. Generally, technicians who work in small-town, family-owned gas stations earn less than those who work at dealerships and franchises in metropolitan areas.

According to the U.S. Department of Labor, automobile service technicians had median annual salaries of $35,100 in 2008. The lowest paid 10 percent made less than $19,890, and the highest paid 10 percent made more than $59,710. Since most technicians are paid on an hourly basis and frequently work overtime, their salaries can vary significantly. In many repair shops and dealerships, technicians can earn higher incomes by working on commission. Master technicians who work on commission can earn more than $100,000 annually. Employers often guarantee a minimum level of pay in addition to commissions.

Benefit packages vary from business to business. Most technicians receive health insurance and paid vacation days. Additional benefits may include dental, life, and disability insurance and a pension plan. Employers usually pay for a technician's work clothes and may pay a percentage on hand tools purchased. An increasing number of employers pay for all or most of an employee's certification training, if he or she passes the test. A technician's salary can increase through yearly bonuses or profit sharing if the business does well.

WORK ENVIRONMENT

Depending on the size of the shop and whether it's an independent or franchised repair shop, dealership, or private business, automobile technicians work with anywhere from two to 20 other technicians. Most shops are well lighted and well ventilated. They can frequently be noisy with running cars and power tools. Minor hand and back injuries are the most common problems of technicians. When reaching in hard-to-get-at places or loosening tight bolts, technicians often bruise, cut, or burn their hands. With caution and experience most technicians learn to avoid hand injuries. Working for long periods of time in cramped or bent positions often results in a stiff back or neck. Technicians also lift many heavy objects that can cause injury if not handled carefully; however, this is becoming less of a problem with new cars, as automakers design smaller and lighter parts to improve fuel economy. Some technicians may experience allergic reactions to solvents and oils used in cleaning, maintenance, and repair. Shops must comply with strict safety procedures set by the Occupational Safety and Health Administration and Environmental Protection Agency to help employees avoid accidents and injuries.

The U.S. Department of Labor reports that most technicians work a standard 40-hour week, but 30 percent of all technicians work more than 40 hours a week. Some technicians make emergency repairs to stranded automobiles on the roadside during odd hours.

OUTLOOK

With an estimated 250 million or more vehicles in operation today, automobile service technicians should feel confident that a good percentage will require servicing and repair. Opportunities will be good for those who complete postsecondary training programs, but those without formal automotive training will face strong competition for entry-level jobs. The U.S. Department of Labor predicts that this field will grow more slowly than the average for all occupations through 2018. According to the ASE, even if school enrollments were at maximum capacity, the demand for automobile service technicians still would exceed the supply in the immediate future. As a result, many shops are beginning to recruit employees while they are still in vocational or even high school.

Most new jobs for technicians will be at independent service dealers and automobile dealerships. However, the restructuring and closing of many automobile dealerships will lead to fewer openings in dealer service centers for the first part of the decade.

Because of the increase of specialty shops, fewer gasoline service stations will hire technicians, and many will eliminate repair services completely. Other opportunities will be available at companies or institutions with private fleets (e.g., cab, delivery, and rental companies, and government agencies and police departments).

Another concern for the industry is the automobile industry's trend toward developing the "maintenance-free" car. Manufacturers are producing high-end cars that require no servicing for their first 100,000 miles. In addition, many new cars are equipped with on-board diagnostics that detect both wear and failure for many of the car's components, eliminating the need for technicians to perform extensive diagnostic tests. Also, parts that are replaced before they completely wear out prevent further damage from occurring to connected parts that are affected by a malfunction or breakdown. Although this will reduce troubleshooting time and the number of overall repairs, the components that need repair will be more costly and require a more experienced (and hence, more expensive) technician.

FOR MORE INFORMATION

For information on accredited training programs, contact
Accrediting Commission of Career Schools and Colleges of Technology
2101 Wilson Boulevard, Suite 302
Arlington, VA 22201-3062
Tel: 703-247-4212
Email: info@accsct.org
http://www.accsct.org

For more information on the automotive service industry, contact
Automotive Aftermarket Industry Association
7101 Wisconsin Avenue, Suite 1300
Bethesda, MD 20814-3415
Tel: 301-654-6664
Email: aaia@aftermarket.org
http://www.aftermarket.org

For information on careers, visit
Automotive Careers Today
http://www.autocareerstoday.net

For industry information and job listings, contact
Automotive Service Association
PO Box 929
Bedford, TX 76095-0929
Tel: 800-272-7467
Email: asainfo@asashop.org
http://www.asashop.org

For information on training and internship opportunities for high school students, visit
Automotive Youth Educational System
https://www.ayes.org

For information and statistics on automotive dealers, contact
National Automobile Dealers Association
8400 Westpark Drive
McLean, VA 22102-5116
Tel: 800-252-6232
Email: nadainfo@nada.org
http://www.nada.org

For information on certified educational programs, careers, and certification, contact
National Automotive Technicians Education Foundation
101 Blue Seal Drive, Suite 101
Leesburg, VA 20175-5646
Tel: 703-669-6650
http://www.natef.org

For information on certification, contact
National Institute for Automotive Service Excellence
101 Blue Seal Drive, Suite 101
Leesburg, VA 20175-5646
Tel: 703-669-6600
http://www.asecert.org

For industry news and updates and general information on biofuels, contact
Renewable Fuels Association
One Massachusetts Avenue, NW, Suite 820
Washington, DC 20001-1401
Tel: 202-289-3835
Email: info@ethanolrfa.org
http://www.ethanolrfa.org

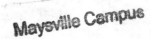

Avionics Technicians

OVERVIEW

Avionics (from the words aviation and electronics) is the application of electronics to the operation of aircraft, spacecraft, and missiles. Avionics technicians inspect, test, adjust, and repair the electronic components of aircraft communications, navigation, and flight-control systems and compile complete maintenance-and-overhaul records for the work they do. Avionics technicians also calibrate and adjust the frequencies of communications apparatus when it is installed and perform periodic checks on those frequency settings. Avionics technicians hold about 18,800 jobs in the United States.

HISTORY

The field of avionics grew out of World War II, when military aircraft were operated for the first time using electronic equipment. Rockets were also being developed during this time, and these devices required electronic systems to control their flight. As aircraft rapidly grew more complicated, the amount of electronic apparatus needed for navigation and for monitoring equipment performance greatly increased. The World War II B-29 bomber carried 2,000 to 3,000 avionic components; the B-52 of the Vietnam era carried 50,000; later, the B-58 supersonic bomber required more than 95,000. As the military grew increasingly reliant on electronic systems, specialists were required to build, install, operate, and repair them.

The development of large ballistic missiles during and after World War II and the rapid growth of the U.S. space program after 1958 increased development of avionics technology. Large missiles and spacecraft require many more electronic components than even the largest and most sophisticated aircraft. Computerized guidance systems became especially important with the advent of manned spaceflights. Avionics technology was also applied to civil aircraft. The race to be the first in space and, later, to be the first to land on the moon, stimulated the need for more and more trained specialists to work with newer and more complex electronic technology. The push for achieving military superiority during the Cold War era also created a demand for avionics specialists and technicians. From the 1950s to the present, the commercial airline industry grew rapidly; more and more planes were being built, and the drive to provide greater comfort and safety for passengers created still greater demand for avionics technicians.

Avionics continues to be an important branch of aeronautical and astronautical engineering. The aerospace industry places great emphasis on research and development, assigning a much higher percentage of its trained technical personnel to this effort than is usual in industry. In addition, stringent safety regulations require constant surveillance of in-service equipment. For these reasons there is a high demand for trained and experienced avionics technicians to help avionics engineers develop new satellites, spacecraft, aircraft, and their component electronic systems and to maintain those in service.

THE JOB

Avionics engineers develop new electronic systems and components for aerospace use. Avionics technicians assist engineers in these developments. They also adapt existing systems and components for application in new equipment. For the most part, however, they install, test, repair, and maintain navigation, communications, and control apparatus in existing aircraft and spacecraft.

Technicians use apparatus such as circuit analyzers and oscilloscopes to test and replace sophisticated equipment, including transceivers and Doppler radar systems, as well as microphones, headsets, and other standard electronic communications apparatus. New equipment, once installed, must be tested and calibrated to prescribed specifications. Technicians also adjust the frequencies of radio sets and other communications equipment by signaling ground stations and then adjusting set screws until the desired frequency has been achieved. Periodic maintenance checks and readjustments enable avionics technicians to keep equipment operating on proper frequencies. Technicians also complete and sign maintenance-and-overhaul documents that record the history of various equipment.

Avionics technicians involved in the design and testing of a new apparatus must take into account all operating conditions, determining weight limitations, resistance to physical shock, the atmospheric conditions the device will have to withstand, and other factors. For some sophisticated projects, technicians will have to design and make their tools first and then use them to construct and test new avionic components.

The range of equipment in the avionics field is so broad that technicians usually specialize in one area, such as radio equipment, radar, computerized guidance, or flight-control systems. New specialty areas are constantly evolving as innovations occur in avionics. The development of these new specialty areas requires technicians to keep informed by reading technical articles and books and by attending seminars and courses about the new developments, which are often sponsored by manufacturers.

Avionics technicians usually work as part of a team, especially if involved in research, testing, and development of new products. They are often required to keep notes and records of their work and to write detailed reports.

REQUIREMENTS

High School

If you are interested in pursuing a career in avionics, you should take high school mathematics courses at least through solid geometry, preferably through calculus. You should also take English, speech, and communication classes in order to read complex and detailed technical articles, books, and reports; to write technical reports; and to present those reports to groups of people when required. Many schools offer shop classes in electronics and in diagram and blueprint reading.

Postsecondary Training

Avionics technicians must have completed a training course at a postsecondary technical institute or community college. The training should include at least one year of electronics technician training. If not trained specifically in avionics, students should obtain a solid background in electronics theory and practice. Further specialized training will be done on the job, where technicians work with engineers and senior technicians until they are competent to work without direct supervision.

Larger corporations in the aerospace industry operate their own schools and training institutes. Such training rarely includes theoretical or general studies but concentrates on areas important to the company's functions. The U.S. Armed Forces also conduct excellent electronics and avionics training schools; their graduates are in high demand in the industry after they leave the service.

Certification or Licensing

The Electronics Technicians Association International (ETA-I) offers four levels of voluntary certification (certified associate, journeyman, senior, and master) for electronics service technicians who wish to specialize in avionics. To become certified, technicians must have a specified number of years of work and/or electronics training and pass an examination. Contact the ETA-I for more information.

Federal Communications Commission (FCC) regulations require that anyone who works with radio transmitting equipment have a restricted radiotelephone operator's license. Such a license is issued upon application to the FCC and is issued for life.

Other Requirements

Students who are thinking about this kind of work should have strong science and mathematics skills. In addition, you will need to

Key Competencies for Avionics Technicians

According to the Electronics Technicians Association International, avionics technicians should have "knowledge and functional abilities" in the following areas:

- Amplifiers
- Antennas and transmission lines
- Avionics systems
- Cables and cabling
- Components
- Computers and digital concepts
- Interfacing
- Mathematics
- Network topologies and infrastructures
- Optical cabling
- People relations
- Safety
- Satellite communications
- Test equipment and tools
- Troubleshooting

have good manual dexterity and mechanical aptitude and the temperament for exacting work.

EXPLORING

One way to learn more about avionics is to visit factories and test facilities where avionics technicians work as part of teams designing and testing new equipment. It is also possible to visit a large airfield's repair facilities where avionics technicians inspect, maintain, and calibrate communications and control apparatus. You can also arrange to visit other types of electronics manufacturers.

Useful information about avionics training programs and career opportunities is available from the U.S. Armed Forces as well as from trade and technical schools and community colleges that offer such programs. These organizations are always pleased to answer inquiries from prospective students or service personnel.

EMPLOYERS

There are approximately 18,800 avionics technicians employed in the United States. Most technicians work for the federal government, aerospace product and parts manufacturing companies, aircraft assembly firms, airlines, or airports.

STARTING OUT

Those entering the field of avionics must first obtain the necessary training in electronics. Following that training, the school's career services office can help locate prospective employers, arrange interviews, and advise about an employment search. Other possibilities are to contact an employment agency or to approach a prospective employer directly. Service in the military is an excellent way to gain education, training, and experience in avionics; many companies are eager to hire technicians with a military background.

ADVANCEMENT

Avionics technicians usually begin their careers in trainee positions until they are thoroughly familiar with the requirements and routines of their work. Having completed their apprenticeships, they are usually assigned to work independently, with only minimal supervision, doing testing and repair work. The most experienced and able technicians go on to install new equipment and to work in research and development operations. Many senior technicians move into training, supervisory, sales, and customer relations positions. Some choose to pursue additional training and become avionics engineers.

EARNINGS

Median earnings of avionics technicians were $49,310 in 2008, according to the U.S. Department of Labor. The top 10 percent of technicians earned more than $64,200 a year. The lowest paid 10 percent earned less than $34,220 a year. Federal government employees (not including armed forces personnel) on average earn slightly less than avionics technicians employed by private aerospace firms. Their jobs, however, are more secure.

Avionics technicians usually receive benefits such as vacation days, sick leave, health and life insurance, and a savings and pension program.

WORK ENVIRONMENT

Avionics technicians work for aircraft and aerospace manufacturers, airlines, and NASA and other government agencies. Most avionics technicians specialize in a specific area of avionics; they are also responsible for keeping up with the latest technological and industry advances. Their work is usually performed in pleasant indoor surroundings. Because this work is very precise, successful technicians must have a personality suited to meeting exact standards and working within small tolerances. Technicians sometimes work in closely cooperating teams. This requires an ability to work with a team spirit of coordinated effort.

OUTLOOK

The U.S. Department of Labor predicts that employment for avionics technicians will grow as fast as the average for all occupations through 2018.

Avionics is an important and constantly developing field for which more and more trained technicians will be needed. Reliance on electronic technology has grown rapidly and in virtually every industry. Many defense contractors have begun to branch out into other products, especially in the areas of electronics and computer technology. Commercial applications of the space program, including the launching of privately owned satellites, are providing new opportunities in the aerospace industry.

The aerospace industry is closely tied to government spending and to political change, as well as to the economy, which also affects the aircraft and airline industries strongly. The cancellation of one spacecraft program or a decline in airline travel that leads to employee cutbacks may throw a large number of avionics technicians out of work, making competition for the remaining jobs very keen.

FOR MORE INFORMATION

For industry information, contact the following organizations:
Aerospace Industries Association
1000 Wilson Boulevard, Suite 1700
Arlington, VA 22209-3928
Tel: 703-358-1000
http://www.aia-aerospace.org

General Aviation Manufacturers Association
1400 K Street, NW, Suite 801
Washington, DC 20005-2485
Tel: 202-393-1500
http://www.gama.aero

For information about avionics careers in Canada, contact
Aerospace Industries Association of Canada
60 Queen Street, Suite 1200
Ottawa, ON K1P 5Y7 Canada
Tel: 613-232-4297
Email: info@aiac.ca
http://www.aiac.ca

For information on careers and student branches, contact
American Institute of Aeronautics and Astronautics
1801 Alexander Bell Drive, Suite 500
Reston, VA 20191-4344
Tel: 800-639-2422
http://www.aiaa.org

For information on certification, contact
Electronics Technicians Association International
Five Depot Street
Greencastle, IN 46135-8024
Tel: 800-288-3824
Email: eta@eta-i.org
http://www.eta-i.org

For information on aviation careers and scholarships, contact
National Air Transportation Association
4226 King Street
Alexandria, VA 22302-1507
Tel: 800-808-6282
http://www.nata.aero

Biomedical Equipment Technicians

OVERVIEW

Biomedical equipment technicians handle the complex medical equipment and instruments found in hospitals, clinics, and research facilities. This equipment is used for medical therapy and diagnosis and includes heart-lung machines, artificial kidney machines, patient monitors, chemical analyzers, and other electrical, electronic, mechanical, or pneumatic devices.

Technicians' main duties are to inspect, maintain, repair, and install this equipment. They disassemble equipment to locate malfunctioning components, repair or replace defective parts, and reassemble the equipment, adjusting and calibrating it to ensure that it operates according to manufacturers' specifications. Biomedical equipment technicians also modify equipment according to the directions of medical or supervisory personnel, arrange with equipment manufacturers for necessary equipment repair, and safety-test equipment to ensure that patients, equipment operators, and other staff members are safe from electrical or mechanical hazards. Biomedical equipment technicians work with hand tools, power tools, measuring devices, and manufacturers' manuals.

Technicians may work for equipment manufacturers as salespeople or as service technicians, or for a health care facility specializing in the repair or maintenance of specific equipment, such as that used in radiology, nuclear medicine, or patient monitoring. In the United States, approximately 41,000 people work as biomedical equipment technicians.

QUICK FACTS

School Subjects
Biology
Technical/shop

Personal Skills
Mechanical/manipulative
Technical/scientific

Work Environment
Primarily indoors
Primarily one location

Minimum Education Level
Associate's degree

Salary Range
$25,860 to $41,520 to $65,930+

Certification or Licensing
Recommended

Outlook
Much faster than the average

DOT
639

GOE
02.05.02

NOC
N/A

O*NET-SOC
49-9062.00, 51-9082.00

HISTORY

Today's complex biomedical equipment is the result of advances in three different areas of engineering and scientific research. The first, of course, is ever-increasing knowledge of the human body and of the disease processes that afflict it. Although the accumulation of medical knowledge has been going on for thousands of years, most of the discoveries leading to the development of medical technology have occurred during the last three hundred years. The past one hundred years, in particular, have seen great advances in knowledge about the chemical and electrical nature of the human body.

The second contribution to biomedical technology's development is the field of instrumentation—the design and building of precision measuring devices. Throughout the history of medicine, physicians and medical researchers have tried to learn about and to monitor the workings of the human body with whatever instruments were available to them. However, it was not until the industrial revolution of the 18th and 19th centuries that instruments were developed that could detect the human body's many subtle and rapid processes.

The third area is mechanization and automation. Biomedical equipment often relies on mechanisms, such as pumps, motors, bellows, control arms, etc. These kinds of equipment were initially developed and improved during the industrial revolution; however, it was not until the 1950s that the field of medical technology began incorporating the use of automation. During the 1950s, researchers developed machines for analyzing the various components of blood and for preparing tissue specimens for microscopic examination. Probably the most dramatic development of this period was the introduction of the heart-lung machine by John Haysham Gibbon of Philadelphia in 1953, a project he had been working on since 1937.

Since the 1950s, the growth of biomedical technology has been especially dramatic. Forty years ago, even the most advanced hospitals had only a few pieces of electronic medical equipment; today such hospitals have thousands. As the person that services this equipment, the biomedical equipment technician has become an important member of the health care delivery team.

In a sense, biomedical equipment technicians represent the newest stage in the history of technicians. The first technicians were skilled assistants who had learned a trade and gone to work for an engineer or scientist. The second generation learned a technology, such as electronics. The most recent generation of technicians needs integrated instruction and competence in at least two fields of science and technology. For the biomedical equipment technician, the fields may vary, but they will most often be electronics and human physiology.

THE JOB

Biomedical equipment technicians are an important link between technology and medicine. They repair, calibrate, maintain, and operate biomedical equipment working under the supervision of researchers, biomedical engineers, physicians, surgeons, and other professional health care providers.

Biomedical equipment technicians may work with thousands of different kinds of equipment. Some of the most frequently encountered are: patient monitors; heart-lung machines; kidney machines; blood-gas analyzers; spectrophotometers; X-ray units; radiation monitors; defibrillators; anesthesia apparatus; pacemakers; blood pressure transducers; spirometers; sterilizers; diathermy equipment; patient-care computers; ultrasound machines; and diagnostic scanning machines, such as the CT (computed tomography) scan machine, PET (positron emission tomography) scanner, and MRI (magnetic resonance imaging) machines.

Repairing faulty instruments is one of the chief functions of biomedical equipment technicians. They investigate equipment problems, determine the extent of malfunctions, make repairs on instruments that have had minor breakdowns, and expedite the repair of instruments with major breakdowns, for instance, by writing an analysis of the problem for the factory. In doing this work, technicians rely on manufacturers' diagrams, maintenance manuals, and standard and specialized test instruments, such as oscilloscopes and pressure gauges.

Installing equipment is another important function of biomedical equipment technicians. They inspect and test new equipment to make sure it complies with performance and safety standards as described in the manufacturer's manuals and diagrams, and as noted on the purchase order. Technicians may also check on proper installation of the equipment, or, in some cases, install it themselves. To ensure safe operations, technicians need a thorough knowledge of the regulations related to the proper grounding of equipment, and they need to actively carry out all steps and procedures to ensure safety.

Maintenance is the third major area of responsibility for biomedical equipment technicians. In doing this work, technicians try to catch problems before they become more serious. To this end, they take apart and reassemble devices, test circuits, clean and oil moving parts, and replace worn parts. They also keep complete records of all machine repairs, maintenance checks, and expenses.

In all three of these areas, a large part of technicians' work consists of consulting with physicians, administrators, engineers, and other related professionals. For example, they may be called upon to assist hospital administrators as they make decisions about the repair, replacement, or purchase of new equipment. They consult with medical and research staff to determine that equipment is functioning safely and properly. They also consult with medical and engineering staffs when called upon to modify or develop equipment. In all of these activities, they use their knowledge of electronics, medical terminology, human anatomy and physiology, chemistry, and physics.

In addition, biomedical equipment technicians are involved in a range of other related duties. Some biomedical equipment technicians maintain inventories of all instruments in the hospital, their condition, location, and operators. They reorder parts and components, assist in providing people with emergency instruments, restore unsafe or defective instruments to working order, and check for safety regulation compliance.

Other biomedical equipment technicians help physicians, surgeons, nurses, and researchers conduct procedures and experiments. In addition, they must be able to explain to staff members how to operate these machines, the conditions under which a certain apparatus may or may not be used, how to solve small operating problems, and how to monitor and maintain equipment.

In many hospitals, technicians are assigned to a particular service, such as pediatrics, surgery, or renal medicine. These technicians become specialists in certain types of equipment. However, unlike electrocardiograph technicians or dialysis technicians, who specialize in one kind of equipment, most biomedical equipment technicians must be thoroughly familiar with a large variety of instruments. They might be called upon to prepare an artificial kidney or to work with a blood-gas analyzer. Biomedical equipment technicians also maintain pulmonary function machines. These machines are used in clinics for ambulatory patients, hospital laboratories, departments of medicine for diagnosis and treatment, and rehabilitation of cardiopulmonary patients.

While most biomedical equipment technicians are trained in electronics technology, there is also a need for technicians trained in plastics to work on the development of artificial organs and for people trained in glass blowing to help make the precision parts for specialized equipment.

Many biomedical equipment technicians work for medical instrument manufacturers. These technicians consult and assist in the construction of new machinery, helping to make decisions concerning materials and construction methods to be used in the manufacture of the equipment.

REQUIREMENTS

High School

There are a number of classes you can take in high school to help you prepare for this work. Science classes such as chemistry, biology, and physics will give you the science background you will need for working in a medical environment. Take shop classes that deal with electronics, drafting, or blueprint reading. These classes will give you experience working with your hands, following printed directions, using electricity, and working with machinery. Mathematics classes will help you become comfortable working with numbers and formulas. Don't neglect your English studies. English classes will help you develop your communication skills, which will be important to have when you deal with a variety of different people in your professional life.

Postsecondary Training

To become qualified for this work, you will need to complete postsecondary education that leads either to an associate's degree from a two-year institution or a bachelor's degree from a four-year college or university. Most biomedical equipment technicians choose to receive an associate's degree. Biomedical equipment technology is a relatively new program in some schools and may also be referred to as *medical electronics technology* or *biomedical engineering technology.* No matter what the name of the program, however, you should expect to receive instruction in such areas as anatomy, physiology, electrical and electronic fundamentals, chemistry, physics, and biomedical equipment construction and design. In addition, you will study safety methods in health care facilities and medical equipment troubleshooting, as it will be your job to be the problem solver. You should also expect to continue taking communication or English classes since communication skills will be essential to your work. In addition to the classroom work, many programs often provide you with practical experience in repairing and servicing equipment in a clinical or laboratory setting under the supervision of an experienced equipment technician. In this way, you learn about electrical components and circuits, the design and construction of common pieces of machinery, and computer technology as it applies to biomedical equipment.

A handful of schools that offer training in biomedical equipment technology are accredited by the Technology Accreditation Commission for the Accreditation Board for Engineering and Technology (http://www.abet.org).

By studying various pieces of equipment, you learn a problem-solving technique that applies not only to the equipment studied, but also to equipment you have not yet seen, and even to equipment that has not yet been invented. Part of this problem-solving technique includes learning how and where to locate sources of information.

Some biomedical equipment technicians receive their training in the armed forces. During the course of an enlistment period of four years or less, military personnel can receive training that prepares them for entry-level or sometimes advanced-level positions in the civilian workforce.

Certification or Licensing
The Board of Examiners for Biomedical Equipment Technicians, which is affiliated with the Association for the Advancement of Medical Instrumentation (AAMI), maintains certification programs for biomedical equipment technicians. The following categories are available: biomedical equipment technician, radiology equipment specialist, and clinical laboratory equipment specialist. Contact the AAMI for more information. Although certification is not required for employment, it is highly recommended. Technicians with certification have demonstrated that they have attained an overall knowledge of the field and are dedicated to their profession. Many employers prefer to hire technicians who are certified.

Other Requirements
Biomedical equipment technicians need mechanical ability and should enjoy working with tools. Because this job demands quick decision making and prompt repairs, technicians should work well under pressure. You should also be extremely precise and accurate in your work, have good communications skills, and enjoy helping others—an essential quality for anyone working in the health care industry.

EXPLORING

You will have difficulty gaining any direct experience in biomedical equipment technology until you are in a training program or working professionally. Your first hands-on opportunities generally come in the clinical and laboratory phases of your education. You can, however, visit school and community libraries to seek out books written about careers in medical technology. You can also join a hobby club devoted to chemistry, biology, radio equipment, or electronics.

Perhaps the best way to learn more about this job is to set up, with the help of teachers or guidance counselors, a visit to a local health care facility or to arrange for a biomedical technician to speak to interested students, either on-site or at a career exploration seminar hosted by the school. You may be able to ask the technician about his or her educational background, what a day on the job is like, and what new technologies are on the horizon. Try to visit a school offering a program in biomedical equipment technology and discuss your career plans with an admissions counselor there. The counselor may also be able to provide you with helpful insights about the career and your preparation for it.

Finally, because this work involves the health care field, consider getting a part-time job or volunteering at a local hospital. Naturally, you won't be asked to work with the biomedical equipment, but you will have the opportunity to see professionals on the job and experience being in the medical environment. Even if your duty is only to escort patients to their tests, you may gain a greater understanding of this work.

EMPLOYERS

Approximately 41,000 biomedical equipment technicians are employed in the United States. Many schools place students in part-time hospital positions to help them gain practical experience. Students are often able to return to these hospitals for full-time employment after graduation. Other places of employment include research institutes, independent service organizations, and biomedical equipment manufacturers. Government hospitals and the military also employ biomedical equipment technicians.

STARTING OUT

Most schools offering programs in biomedical equipment technology work closely with local hospitals and industries, and school career services counselors are usually informed about openings when they become available. In some cases, recruiters may visit a school periodically to conduct interviews. Also, many schools place students in part-time hospital jobs to help them gain practical experience. Students are often able to return to these hospitals for full-time employment after graduation.

Another effective method of finding employment is to write directly to hospitals, research institutes, or biomedical equipment manufacturers. Other good sources of leads for job openings include state employment offices and newspaper want ads.

ADVANCEMENT

With experience, biomedical equipment technicians can expect to work with less supervision, and in some cases they may find themselves supervising less-experienced technicians. They may advance to positions in which they serve as instructors, assist in research, or have administrative duties. Although many supervisory positions are open to biomedical equipment technicians, some positions are not available without additional education. In large metropolitan hospitals, for instance, the minimum educational requirement for biomedical engineers, who do much of the supervising of biomedical equipment technicians, is a bachelor's degree; many engineers have a master's degree as well.

EARNINGS

Salaries for biomedical equipment technicians vary in different institutions and localities and according to the experience, training, certification, and type of work done by the technician. According to the U.S. Department of Labor, the median annual salary for medical equipment repairers was $41,520 in 2008. The top paid 10 percent of workers in this profession made $65,930 or more a year, while the lowest paid 10 percent made $25,860 or less per year. In general, biomedical equipment technicians who work for manufacturers have higher earnings than those who work for hospitals. Naturally, those in supervisory or senior positions also command higher salaries. Benefits, such as health insurance and vacation days, vary with the employer.

WORK ENVIRONMENT

Working conditions for biomedical equipment technicians vary according to employer and type of work done. Hospital employees generally work a 40-hour week; their schedules sometimes include weekends and holidays, and some technicians may be on call for emergencies. Technicians who are employed by equipment manufacturers may have to travel extensively to install or service equipment.

The physical surroundings in which biomedical equipment technicians work may vary from day to day. Technicians may work in a lab or treatment room with patients or consult with engineers, administrators, and other staff members. Other days, technicians may spend most of their time at a workbench repairing equipment.

OUTLOOK

Because of the expanding health care field and increasing use of electronic medical devices and other sophisticated biomedical equipment, there is a steady demand for skilled and trained biomedical equipment technicians. The U.S. Department of Labor predicts that employment for these workers will grow much faster than the average for all occupations through 2018.

In hospitals the need for more biomedical equipment technicians exists not only because of the increasing use of biomedical equipment but also because hospital administrators realize that these technicians can help hold down costs. Biomedical equipment technicians do this through their preventive maintenance checks and by taking over some routine activities of engineers and administrators, thus releasing those professionals for activities that only they can perform. Through the coming decades, cost containment will remain a high priority for hospital administrators, and as long as biomedical equipment technicians can contribute to that effort, the demand for them should remain strong.

Job opportunities should also continue to grow for the many biomedical equipment technicians who work for companies that build, sell, lease, or service biomedical equipment.

The federal government employs biomedical equipment technicians in its hospitals, research institutes, and the military. Employment in these areas will depend largely on levels of government spending. In the research area, spending levels may vary; however, in health care delivery, spending should remain high for the near future.

FOR MORE INFORMATION

For industry information, contact
American Society for Healthcare Engineering
One North Franklin, 28th Floor
Chicago, IL 60606-4425
Tel: 312-422-3800
Email: ashe@aha.org
http://www.ashe.org

For information on student memberships, biomedical technology programs, and certification, contact
Association for the Advancement of Medical Instrumentation
1110 North Glebe Road, Suite 220
Arlington, VA 22201-4795
Tel: 703-525-4890
Email: certifications@aami.org
http://www.aami.org

For information on careers, contact
Medical Equipment and Technology Association
http://www.mymeta.org

Chemical Technicians

OVERVIEW

Chemical technicians assist chemists and chemical engineers in the research, development, testing, and manufacturing of chemicals and chemical-based products. Approximately 66,000 chemical technicians work in the United States.

HISTORY

The practice of modern chemistry goes back thousands of years to when humans first extracted medicinal substances from plants and shaped metals into tools and utensils for daily life. In the late 18th century, chemistry became established as a science when Antoine Lavoisier formulated the law of the conservation of matter. From that time until the present, the number and types of products attributed to the development and expansion of chemistry are almost incalculable.

The period following World War I was a time of enormous expansion of chemical technology and its application to the production of goods and consumer products such as high octane gasoline, antifreeze, pesticides, pharmaceuticals, plastics, and artificial fibers and fabrics. This rapid expansion increased the need for professionally trained chemists and technicians. The technicians, with their basic chemical knowledge and manual skills, were able to handle the tasks that did not require the specialized education of their bosses. These nonprofessionals sometimes had the title of junior chemist.

During the last 30 years, however, there has been a radical change in the status of the chemical technician from a "mere" assistant to a core professional. Automation and computerization have increased

42

laboratory efficiency, and corporate downsizing has eliminated many layers of intermediate hierarchy. The result has been to increase the level of responsibility and independence, meaning greater recognition of the importance of today's highly skilled and trained chemical technicians.

THE JOB

Most chemical technicians who work in the chemical industry are involved in the development, testing, and manufacturing of plastics, paints, detergents, synthetic fibers, industrial chemicals, and pharmaceuticals. Others work in the petroleum, aerospace, metals, electronics, automotive, and construction industries. Some chemical technicians work in universities and government laboratories.

They may work in any of the fields of chemistry, such as analytical, biochemistry, inorganic, organic, physical, or any of the many sub-branches of chemistry. Chemical engineering, which is a combination of chemistry and engineering, develops or improves manufacturing processes for making commercial amounts of chemicals, many of which were previously produced only in small quantities in laboratory glassware or a pilot plant.

Within these subfields, chemical technicians work in research and development, design and production, and quality control. In research and development, chemical laboratory technicians often work with chemists and chemical engineers to set up and monitor laboratory equipment and instruments, prepare laboratory setups, and record data.

Technicians often determine the chemical composition, concentration, stability, and level of purity on a wide range of materials. These may include ores, minerals, pollutants, foods, drugs, plastics, dyes, paints, detergents, chemicals, paper, and petroleum products. Although chemists or chemical engineers may design an experiment, technicians help them create process designs, develop written procedures, or devise computer simulations. They also select all necessary glassware, reagents, chemicals, and equipment. Technicians also perform analyses and report test results.

In the design and production area, chemical technicians work closely with chemical engineers to monitor the large-scale production of compounds and to help develop and improve the processes and equipment used. They prepare tables, charts, sketches, diagrams, and flowcharts that record and summarize the collected data. They work with pipelines, valves, pumps, and metal and glass tanks. Chemical technicians often use their input to answer manufacturing questions, such as how to transfer materials from one point to another, and to build, install, modify, and maintain processing equipment. They also train and supervise production operators. They may operate small-scale equipment for determining process parameters.

Fuel technicians determine viscosities of oils and fuels, measure flash points (the temperature at which fuels catch fire), pour points (the coldest temperature at which the fuel can flow), and the heat output of fuels.

Pilot plant operators make erosion and corrosion tests on new construction materials to determine their suitability. They prepare chemicals for field testing and report on the effectiveness of new design concepts.

Applied research technicians help design new manufacturing or research equipment.

REQUIREMENTS

High School
You should take several years of science and mathematics in high school. Computer training is also important. While a minority of employers still hire high school graduates and place them into their own training programs, the majority prefer to hire graduates of community colleges who have completed two-year chemical technician programs or even bachelor degree recipients. If you plan on attending a four-year college, take three years of high school mathematics, including algebra, geometry, and trigonometry; three years of physical sciences, including chemistry; and four years of English.

Postsecondary Training
Graduates of community college programs are productive much sooner than untrained individuals because they have the technical knowledge, laboratory experience, and skills for the job. Computer courses are necessary, as computers and computer-interfaced equipment are routinely used in the field. Realizing that many students become aware of technical career possibilities too late to satisfy college requirements, many community and technical colleges that offer chemical technician programs may also have noncredit courses that allow students to meet college entrance requirements.

Approximately 150 two-year colleges in the United States have chemistry or chemical technology programs. Once enrolled in a two-year college program designed for chemical technicians, students should expect to take a number of chemistry courses with strong emphasis on laboratory work and the presentation of data. These courses include basic concepts of modern chemistry, such as atomic structure, descriptive chemistry of both organic and inorganic substances, analytical methods including quantitative and instrumental analysis, and physical properties of substances. Other courses include communications, physics, mathematics, industrial safety, and organic laboratory equipment and procedures. Chemical technicians who work in research and development may need a bachelor's degree.

Other Requirements

Besides the educational requirements, certain personal characteristics are necessary for successful chemical technicians. You must have both the ability and the desire to use mental and manual skills. You should also have a good supply of patience because experiments must frequently be repeated several times. You should be precise and like doing detailed work. Mechanical aptitude and good powers of observation are also needed. You should be able to follow directions closely and enjoy solving problems. Chemical technicians also need excellent organizational and communication skills. Other important qualities are a desire to learn new skills and a willingness to accept responsibility. In addition, you should have good eyesight, color perception, and hand-eye coordination.

The American Chemical Society (ACS) maintains a database of skill standards for chemical technicians at its Web site (http://www.chemistry.org).

EXPLORING

You can explore this field by joining high school science clubs or organizations and taking part in extracurricular activities offered by the Junior Engineering Technical Society (JETS). Science contests are a good way to apply principles learned in classes to a special project. You can also subscribe to the ACS's *ChemMatters,* a quarterly magazine for students taking chemistry in high school. Examples of topics covered in the magazine include the chemistry of lipstick, suntan products, contact lenses, and carbon-14 dating. Also, qualifying students can participate in Project SEED (Summer Education Experience for the Disadvantaged), a summer program designed to provide high school students from economically disadvantaged homes with the opportunity to experience science research in a laboratory environment. (Visit http://www.chemistry.org for more information.)

Once you are in college, you can join the student affiliates of professional associations such as the ACS and the American Institute of Chemical Engineers (AIChE). Membership allows students

Books to Read: Chemistry Experiments

Garland, Carl W., Joseph W. Nibler, and David P. Shoemaker. *Experiments in Physical Chemistry.* 8th ed. New York: McGraw-Hill Higher Education, 2008.

Herr, Norman, and James Cunningham. *Hands-On Chemistry Activities with Real-Life Applications: Easy-to-Use Labs and Demonstrations for Grades 8-12.* San Francisco: Jossey-Bass, 1999.

Murov, Steven, and Brian Stedjee. *Experiments and Exercises in Basic Chemistry.* 5th ed. Florence, Ky.: Brooks Cole, 2006.

Roesky, Herbert W., and George A. Olah. *Spectacular Chemical Experiments.* Weinheim, Germany: Wiley-VCH, 2007.

Rohrig, Brian. *150 Captivating Chemistry Experiments Using Household Substances.* Rev. ed. Plain City, Ohio: FizzBang Science, 2002.

Rohrig, Brian. *150 More Captivating Chemistry Experiments Using Household Substances.* Plain City, Ohio: FizzBang Science, 2002.

Wentworth, Rupert. *Experiments in General Chemistry.* 8th ed. Boston: Houghton Mifflin Company, 2006.

to experience the professionalism of a career in chemistry. You can also contact ACS or AIChE local sections to talk with chemists and chemical engineers about what they do. These associations may also help students find summer or co-op work experiences.

EMPLOYERS

Almost all chemical laboratories, no matter their size or function, employ chemical technicians to assist their chemists or chemical engineers with research as well as routine laboratory work. Therefore, chemical technicians can find employment wherever chemistry is involved: in industrial laboratories, in government agencies such as the Department of Health and Human Services and the Department of Agriculture, and at colleges and universities. They can work in almost any field of chemical activity, such as industrial manufacturing of all kinds, pharmaceuticals, food, and production of chemicals. There are approximately 66,000 chemical technicians currently employed in the United States. Approximately 39 percent work in chemical manufacturing and 30 percent work in technical, professional, or scientific services firms.

STARTING OUT

Graduates of chemical technology programs often find jobs during the last term of their two-year programs. Some companies work with local community colleges and technical schools to maintain a supply of trained chemical technicians. Recruiters regularly visit most colleges where chemical technology programs are offered. Most employers recruit locally or regionally. Because companies hire locally and work closely with technical schools, career services offices are usually successful in finding jobs for their graduates.

Some recruiters also go to four-year colleges and look for chemists with bachelor's degrees. Whether a company hires bachelor's-level chemists or two-year chemical technology graduates depends on both the outlook of the company and the local supply of graduates.

Internships and co-op work are highly regarded by employers, and participation in such programs is a good way to get your foot in the door. Many two- and four-year schools have co-op programs in which full-time students work approximately 20 hours a week for a local company. Such programs may be available to high school seniors as well. Students in these programs develop a good knowledge of the employment possibilities and frequently stay with their co-op employers.

More and more companies are using contract workers to perform technicians' jobs, and this is another way to enter the field. There are local agencies that place technicians with companies for special projects or temporary assignments that last anywhere from a month to a year or more. Many of these contract workers are later hired on a full-time basis.

The ACS Web site (http://www.chemistry.org) is an excellent resource for job seekers. It provides job listings, tips on interviewing and resumes, and information on internships and its mentorship program for members.

ADVANCEMENT

Competent chemical technicians can expect to have long-term career paths. Top research and development positions are open to technically trained people, whether they start out with an associate's degree in chemical technology, a bachelor's degree in chemistry, or just a lot of valuable experience with no degree. There are also opportunities for advancement in the areas of technology development and technology management, providing comparable pay for these separate but equal paths. Some companies have the same career path for all technicians, regardless of education level. Other companies have different career ladders for technicians and chemists but will promote qualified technicians to chemists and move them up that path.

Some companies may require additional formal schooling for promotion, and the associate's degree can be a stepping-stone toward a bachelor's degree in chemistry. Many companies encourage their technicians to continue their education, and most reimburse tuition costs. Continuing education in the form of seminars, workshops, and in-company presentations is also important for advancement. Chemical technicians who want to advance must keep up with current developments in the field by reading trade and technical journals and publications.

EARNINGS

Earnings for chemical technicians vary based on their education, experience, employer, and location. The U.S. Department of Labor reports that the median wage for chemical technicians was $42,120 in 2008. The top paid 10 percent earned $64,650 or more, while the lowest paid 10 percent earned $26,170 or less. Salaries tend to be highest in private industry and lowest in colleges and universities.

If a technician belongs to a union, his or her wages and benefits depend on the union agreement. However, the percentage of technicians who belong to a union is very small. Benefits depend on the employer, but they usually include paid vacations and holidays, insurance, and tuition refund plans. Technicians normally work a five-day, 40-hour week. Occasional overtime may be necessary.

WORK ENVIRONMENT

Although chemical technicians sometimes work with toxic chemicals or radioactive isotopes, the chemical industry is one of the safest industries in which to work. Laboratories and plants normally have safety committees and safety engineers who closely monitor equipment and practices to minimize hazards. Chemical technicians usually receive safety training both in school and at work to recognize potential hazards and to take appropriate measures.

Most chemical laboratories are clean and well lighted. Technicians often work at tables and benches while operating laboratory equipment and are usually provided office or desk space to record data and prepare reports. The work can sometimes be monotonous and repetitive, as when making samples or doing repetitive testing.

Chemical plants are usually clean, and the number of operating personnel for the space involved is often very low.

Chemical technicians typically work a standard 40-hour week, but shifts may be scheduled on weekends and around the clock.

OUTLOOK

The U.S. Department of Labor expects employment for chemical technicians to experience little or no change through 2018, as a result of downsizing and outsourcing by chemical manufacturers. Despite this prediction, chemical technicians will still be needed as the medicine and pharmaceutical manufacturing industries work to improve and produce new medicines and personal care products. Chemical technicians will also be needed by businesses that provide environmental services and "earth-friendly" products, analytical development and services, custom or niche products and services, and quality control.

Graduates of chemical technology programs will continue to face competition from bachelor's-level chemists. The chemical and chemical-related industries will continue to become increasingly sophisticated in both their products and their manufacturing techniques. Technicians trained to deal with automation and complex production methods will have the best employment opportunities.

FOR MORE INFORMATION

For general career information, as well as listings of chemical technology programs, internships, and summer job opportunities, contact

American Chemical Society
1155 16th Street, NW
Washington, DC 20036-4839
Tel: 800-227-5558
Email: help@acs.org
http://www.chemistry.org

The American Chemistry Council offers a great deal of information about the chemical industry, and maintains an informative Web site.

American Chemistry Council
1300 Wilson Boulevard
Arlington, VA 22209-2323
Tel: 703-741-5000
http://www.americanchemistry.com

For information on awards, student chapters, and career opportunities, contact
American Institute of Chemical Engineers
Three Park Avenue
New York, NY 10016-5991
Tel: 800-242-4363
http://www.aiche.org

For information about programs, products, and a chemical engineering career brochure, contact
Junior Engineering Technical Society
1420 King Street, Suite 405
Alexandria, VA 22314-2750
Tel: 703-548-5387
Email: info@jets.org
http://www.jets.org

For fun and educational information on the field of chemistry, check out the following Web site:
Rader's CHEM4KIDS!
http://www.chem4kids.com

Computer and Office Machine Service Technicians

OVERVIEW

Computer and office machine service technicians install, calibrate, maintain, troubleshoot, and repair equipment such as computers and their peripherals, office equipment, and specialized electronic equipment used in many factories, hospitals, airplanes, and numerous other businesses. Computer and office machine service technicians, including those who work on automated teller machines, hold approximately 153,000 jobs in the United States.

HISTORY

When computers were first introduced to the business world, they were very large and cumbersome, and their capabilities were limited. Today, technological advances have made computers significantly smaller yet more powerful in their speed and capabilities. As more businesses rely on computers and other office machines to help manage daily activities, access information, and link offices and resources, the need for experienced professionals to work and service these machines will increase. Service technicians are employed by many corporations, hospitals, and the government, as part of a permanent staff, or they may be contracted to work for other businesses.

QUICK FACTS

School Subjects
Computer science
Technical/shop

Personal Skills
Mechanical/manipulative
Technical/scientific

Work Environment
Primarily indoors
Primarily multiple locations

Minimum Education Level
Associate's degree

Salary Range
$23,180 to $37,810 to $59,100+

Certification or Licensing
Recommended

Outlook
Decline

DOT
633

GOE
05.02.02

NOC
2242

O*NET-SOC
49-2011.00, 49-2011.02, 49-2011.03

THE JOB

Computer and office machine service technicians install and repair personal, mainframe, and server computers; printers; and auxiliary computer equipment, as well as copy machines, fax machines, and other office equipment. There are two main types of technicians: field technicians and bench technicians.

A technician repairs a laptop computer. *(Sarah-Maria Vischer, The Image Works)*

Field technicians are employed either by a specialty repair shop, machine manufacturer, or product-specific service company. They travel to the client's workplace to perform maintenance and repairs. Their duties include following a predetermined schedule of maintenance. For example, they might change the toner, make mechanical adjustments, or clean the optic parts in photocopiers and printers. They also respond to requests for emergency service, since poorly performing equipment can cost a company money and lost productivity. Technicians must also maintain detailed records of service and repairs that they have made in order to address future problems more effectively.

At times, computers may require major repairs that are too complicated to be handled in the office or workplace. In this instance, a field technician takes the computer to a repair shop or company service area to be worked on by *bench servicers,* that is, technicians who work at their employer's location.

Some very experienced computer and office machine servicers open their own repair shops. To remain competitive, they may have to service a wide range of equipment in order to be successful or sell complementary products such as paper and toner for printers, fax machines, and photocopiers. In addition to technical skills, these entrepreneurs need knowledge of the basics of running a business, including bookkeeping and advertising.

REQUIREMENTS

High School
High school courses such as mathematics, physical sciences, and other laboratory-based sciences can provide a strong foundation for understanding basic mechanical and electronics principles. English and speech classes can help boost your written and verbal communication skills. Shop classes dealing with electricity, electronics, and blueprint reading are also beneficial. Computer science classes, of course, will provide you with great experience working with computer hardware and software.

Postsecondary Training
You may be able to find work with a high school diploma if you have a lot of practical, hands-on experience in the field. Usually, however, employers require job candidates to have at least an associate's degree in electronics.

Certification or Licensing
Most employers require certification, though standards vary depending on the company. However many consider certification

as a measure of industry knowledge. Certification can also give you a competitive edge when interviewing for a new job or negotiating for a higher salary.

A variety of certification programs are available from the International Society of Certified Electronics Technicians, ACES International, the Institute for Certification of Computing Professionals, CompTIA, Electronics Technicians Association International, among other organizations. (See For More Information at the end of this article.) After the successful completion of study and examination, you may be certified in fields such as computer, industrial, and electronic equipment. Continuing education credits are required for recertification, usually every two to four years.

Other Requirements

A strong technical background and an aptitude for learning about new technologies, good communication skills, and superior manual dexterity will help you succeed in this industry. You'll also need to be motivated to keep up with modern computer and office machine technology. Machines rapidly become obsolete, and so does the service technician's training. When new equipment is installed, service technicians must demonstrate the intellectual agility to learn how to handle problems that might arise.

EXPLORING

A great way to learn more about this career is by watching a technician at work as he or she repairs computers and office equipment at your school or in your home. You can also ask your school counselor to arrange a presentation or information interview with a technician. Learning the basics (toner replacement, fixing paper jams, etc.) of maintaining a copier or printer will also give you a good introduction to the field.

EMPLOYERS

Approximately 153,000 computer and office machine service technicians, including those who work on automated teller machines, are employed in the United States. Potential employers include computer companies and large corporations that need a staff devoted to repairing and maintaining their equipment; electronics, appliance, and office supply stores; electronic and precision equipment repair shops; computer systems design firms; government agencies; and Internet service providers. Many service technicians are employed by companies that contract their services to other businesses. Though work opportunities for service technicians are available nationwide, many jobs are located in large cities where computer companies and larger corporations are based. Approximately 20 percent of computer and office machine service technicians are self-employed.

STARTING OUT

If your school offers placement services, take advantage of them. Many times, school career services and counseling centers are privy to job openings that are filled before being advertised in the newspaper. Make sure your counselors know of any important preferences, such as location, specialization, and other requirements, so they can best match you to an employer. Do not forget to supply your counselors with an updated resume.

There are also other avenues to take when searching for a job in this industry. Many jobs are advertised in the "Jobs" section of your local newspaper. Look under "Computers" or "Electronics." Also, inquire directly with the personnel department of companies that appeal to you and fill out an application. Trade association Web sites are good sources of job leads; many will post employment opportunities as well as allow you to post your resume.

ADVANCEMENT

Due to the growth of computer products and their influence over the business world, this industry offers a variety of advancement opportunities. Service technicians usually start by working on relatively simple maintenance and repair tasks. Over time, they start working on more complicated projects.

Experienced service technicians may advance to positions of increased responsibility, such as a crew supervisor or a departmental manager. Another advancement route is to become a sales representative for a computer manufacturing company. Technicians develop hands-on knowledge of particular machines and are thus often in the best position to advise potential buyers about important purchasing decisions. Some entrepreneurial-minded servicers might open their own repair business, which can be risky but can also provide many rewards. Unless they fill a certain market niche, technicians usually find it necessary to service a wide range of computers and office machines.

EARNINGS

The U.S. Department of Labor reports that the median hourly earnings for computer, automated teller, and office machine technicians were $18.18 in 2008. A technician earning this amount and working full time would have a yearly income of approximately $37,810. The department also reports that the lowest paid 10 percent of all computer and office machine service technicians (regardless of employer) earned less than $11.14 per hour ($23,180 annually). At the other end of the pay scale, 10 percent earned more than $28.41 per hour (approximately $59,100 annually). Those with certification are typically paid more than those without.

Standard work benefits for full-time technicians include health and life insurance and paid vacation and sick time, as well as a retirement plan. Most technicians are given travel stipends; some receive company cars.

WORK ENVIRONMENT

Most service technicians have unpredictable work schedules. Some weeks are quiet and may require fewer work hours. However, during a major computer problem, or worse yet, a breakdown, technicians are required to work around the clock to fix the problem as quickly as possible. Technicians spend a considerable amount of time on call and must carry a pager in case of work emergencies.

Travel is an integral part of the job for many service technicians, many times amounting to 80 percent of the job time.

OUTLOOK

According to the U.S. Department of Labor, employment for service technicians working with computer and office equipment is expected to decline through 2018. Despite this prediction, demand for qualified and skilled technicians will be steady as corporations, the government, hospitals, and universities worldwide continue to rely on computers to manage their daily business. Opportunities are expected to be best for those with knowledge of electronics and computer repairs. Those working on office equipment, such as digital copiers, should find a demand for their services to repair and maintain increasingly technically sophisticated office machines.

FOR MORE INFORMATION

For industry and certification information, contact the following organizations:

ACES International
5381 Chatham Lake Drive
Virginia Beach, VA 23464-5400

Tel: 757-499-2850
Email: aces@acesinternational.org
http://www.acesinternational.org

CompTIA
1815 South Meyers Road, Suite 300
Oakbrook Terrace, IL 60181-5228
Tel: 630-678-8300
http://www.comptia.org

Institute for Certification of Computing Professionals
2400 East Devon Avenue, Suite 281
Des Plaines, IL 60018-4629
Tel: 800-843-8227
Email: office@iccp.org
http://www.iccp.org

International Society of Certified Electronics Technicians
3608 Pershing Avenue
Fort Worth, TX 76107-4527
Tel: 800-946-0201
Email: info@iscet.org
http://www.iscet.org

For information on internships, student membership, and the magazine Crossroads, *contact*
Association for Computing Machinery
Two Penn Plaza, Suite 701
New York, NY 10121-0701
Tel: 800-342-6626
Email: sigs@acm.org
http://www.acm.org

For information on certification, contact
Electronics Technicians Association International
Five Depot Street
Greencastle, IN 46135-8024
Tel: 800-288-3824
Email: eta@eta-i.org
http://www.eta-i.org

Engineering Technicians

QUICK FACTS

School Subjects
Computer science
Mathematics
Physics

Personal Skills
Mechanical/manipulative
Technical/scientific

Work Environment
Indoors and outdoors
One location with some
    travel

Minimum Education Level
Some postsecondary training

Salary Range
$26,000 to $48,000 to
    $80,000+

Certification or Licensing
Recommended

Outlook
More slowly than the average

DOT
003, 005, 007, 008, 012,
    013

GOE
02.08.04

NOC
2211, 2212, 2223, 2231,
    2232, 2233, 2254

O*NET-SOC
17-3021.00, 17-3022.00,
    17-3023.01, 17-3023.02,
    17-3023.03, 17-3024.00,
    17-3025.00, 17-3026.00,
    17-3027.00, 17-3029.99

OVERVIEW

Engineering technicians use engineering, science, and mathematics to help engineers and other professionals in research and development, quality control, manufacturing, and many other fields. Approximately 497,000 engineering technicians are employed in the United States.

HISTORY

Engineering technicians assist engineers, scientists, and other workers in a variety of tasks. They are highly trained workers with strong backgrounds in a specialized technological field, such as aerospace, civil, materials, and many other types of engineering. In short, engineering technicians can be found supporting engineers and other workers in any engineering discipline that comes to mind. They bridge the gap between the engineers who design the products, structures, and machines, and those who implement them. Engineering technicians have been valuable members of the engineering team ever since the first engineering projects were envisioned, planned, and implemented.

THE JOB

You may not know it, but engineering technicians play a role in almost every part of our daily lives. We can thank engineering technicians (along with engineers, scientists, and other workers) for safer cars and planes, drugs that work effectively when we are sick, well-constructed buildings and highways, clean water and air, and the computer games we play for hours, among many other things.

Some of the major technician specialties include electrical and electronics engineering, civil engineering, industrial engineering, and mechanical engineering. The following paragraphs provide more information on these and other engineering technician specialties.

Aeronautical and aerospace engineering technicians design, construct, test, operate, and maintain the basic structures of aircraft and spacecraft, as well as propulsion and control systems. They work with scientists and aeronautical aerospace engineers. Many aeronautical and aerospace engineering technicians assist engineers in preparing equipment drawings, diagrams, blueprints, and scale models. They collect information, make computations, and perform laboratory tests.

Biomedical engineering technicians use engineering and life science principles to help biomedical engineers and scientists research biological aspects of animal and human life. They help design and construct health care instruments and devices and apply engineering principles to the study of human systems.

Chemical engineering technicians assist chemists and chemical engineers in the research, development, testing, and manufacturing of chemicals and chemical-based products.

Civil engineering technicians help civil engineers design, plan, and build public and private works to meet the community's needs. Civil engineers and technicians work together for the community, providing better, faster transportation; designing and developing highways, airports, and railroads; improving the environment; and constructing buildings, bridges, and space platforms. These engineering professionals work in one of the seven main civil engineering areas: structural, geotechnical, environmental, water resources, transportation, construction, and urban and community planning. The work is closely related, so a technician might work in one, or many, of these areas. A variety of subspecialties are available, including structural engineering technicians, geotechnical engineering technicians, materials technicians, urban and community planning technicians, research engineering technicians, sales engineering, transportation technicians, highway technicians, rail and waterway technicians, and construction engineering technicians.

Electrical and electronics engineering technicians work individually or with engineers to help design, produce, improve, maintain, test, and repair a wide range of electronic equipment. Equipment varies from consumer goods like televisions, computers, and home

Engineering technicians must have excellent technical skills, be highly organized, and be attentive to detail. *(Bob Daemmrich, The Image Works)*

entertainment components, to industrial, military, and medical systems, such as radar and laser equipment. Electronic devices play a part in practically every business and in many leisure activities found around the globe. Such diverse activities as NASA space missions, sophisticated medical testing procedures, and car and airplane travel would be impossible without the use of electronic equipment. The products made by the electronics industry can be divided into four basic categories: government products (which includes missile and space guidance systems, communications systems, medical technology, and traffic control devices), industrial products (which includes large-scale computers, radio and television broadcasting equipment, telecommunications equipment, and electronic office equipment), consumer products (which includes televisions, DVD and MP3 players, and radios), and components (which comprises the smaller pieces that make up all electronics, such as capacitors, switches, transistors, relays, and amplifiers). Subspecialties in this career field include electronics development technicians, electronics drafters, cost-estimating technicians, electronics manufacturing and production technicians, and electronics service and maintenance technicians.

Environmental engineering technicians help environmental engineers and scientists design, build, and maintain systems to control waste streams produced by municipalities or private industry.

Environmental engineering technicians typically focus on one of three areas: air, land, or water.

Industrial engineering technicians assist industrial engineers in their duties: they collect and analyze data and make recommendations for the efficient use of personnel, materials, and machines to produce goods or to provide services. They may study the time, movements, and methods a worker uses to accomplish daily tasks in production, maintenance, or clerical areas. The kind of work done by industrial engineering technicians varies, depending on the size and type of company for which they work. A variety of subspecialties are available, including methods engineering technicians, materials handling technicians, plant layout technicians, work measurement technicians, time-study technicians, production-control technicians, and inventory control technicians.

Materials engineering technicians work in support of materials engineers and scientists. These jobs involve the production, quality control, and experimental study of metals, ceramics, glass, plastics, semiconductors, and composites (combinations of these materials). Metallurgical technicians may conduct tests on the properties of the aforementioned materials, develop and modify test procedures and equipment, analyze data, and prepare reports.

Mechanical engineering technicians work under the direction of mechanical engineers to design, build, maintain, and modify many kinds of machines, mechanical devices, and tools. They work in a wide range of industries and in a variety of specific jobs within every industry. Technicians may specialize in any one of many areas, including biomedical equipment, measurement and control, products manufacturing, solar energy, turbo machinery, energy resource technology, and engineering materials and technology.

Petroleum engineering technicians help petroleum engineers and scientists improve petroleum drilling technology, maximize field production, and provide technical assistance.

Robotics technicians assist robotics engineers in a wide variety of tasks relating to the design, development, production, testing, operation, repair, and maintenance of robots and robotic devices.

Engineering technicians work in a variety of conditions depending on their field of specialization. Technicians who specialize in design may find that they spend most of their time at the drafting board or computer. Those who specialize in manufacturing may spend some time at a desk but also spend considerable time in manufacturing areas or shops.

Conditions also vary according to industry. Some industries require technicians to work in foundries, die-casting rooms, machine shops, assembly areas, or punch-press areas. Most of these areas, however, are well lighted, heated, and ventilated. Moreover, most industries employing engineering technicians have strong safety programs.

REQUIREMENTS
High School
Preparation for this career begins in high school. Although entrance requirements to associate's degree programs vary somewhat from school to school, mathematics and physical science form the backbone of a good college preparatory curriculum. Classes should include algebra, geometry, science, trigonometry, calculus, chemistry, mechanical drawing, shop, and physics. Because computers have become essential for engineering technicians, computer courses are also important.

English and speech courses provide invaluable experience in improving verbal and written communication skills. Since some technicians go on to become technical writers or teachers, and since all of them need to be able to explain technical matter clearly and concisely, communication skills are important.

Postsecondary Training
While some current engineering technicians enter the field without formal academic training, it is increasingly difficult to do so. Most employers are interested in hiring graduates with at least a two-year degree in engineering technology. Technical institutes, community colleges, vocational schools, and universities offer this course of study.

The Technology Accreditation Commission of the Accreditation Board for Engineering and Technology (http://www.abet.org) accredits engineering technology programs.

Some engineering technicians decide to pursue advancement in their field by becoming engineering technologists. Others decide to branch off into research and development or become engineers. These higher-level and higher-paid positions typically require the completion of a bachelor's degree in engineering technology (for engineering technologists) or at least a bachelor's degree in engineering (for technicians interested in working in research and development or becoming engineers).

Certification or Licensing
Certification and licensing requirements vary by specialty. Check with your state's department of labor and professional associations within your field for further information.

Many engineering technicians choose to become certified by the National Institute for Certification in Engineering Technologies. To become certified, you must combine a specific amount of job-related experience with a written examination. Certifications are offered at several levels of expertise. Such certification is generally voluntary, although obtaining certification shows a high level of commitment and dedication that employers find highly desirable.

Electronics engineering technicians may obtain voluntary certification from the International Society of Certified Electronics Technicians and the Electronics Technicians Association International. This certification is regarded as a demonstration of professional dedication, determination, and know-how.

Engineering technicians are encouraged to become affiliated with professional groups, such as the American Society of Certified Engineering Technicians, that offer continuing education sessions for members. Additionally, some engineering technicians may be required to belong to unions.

Other Requirements

All engineering technicians are relied upon for solutions and must express their ideas clearly in speech and in writing. Good communication skills are important for a technician in the writing and presenting of reports and plans. These skills are also important for working alongside other technicians and professionals, people who are often from many different backgrounds and skilled in varying areas of engineering.

Books to Read

Burroughs, Andrew. *Everyday Engineering: What Engineers See.* San Francisco: Chronicle Books, 2007.

Davidson, Frank P., and Kathleen Lusk Brooke. *Building the World: An Encyclopedia of the Great Engineering Projects in History.* Santa Barbara, Calif.: Greenwood Press, 2006.

Landels, John G. *Engineering in the Ancient World.* Rev. ed. Berkeley, Calif.: University of California Press, 2000.

McGraw-Hill. *Dictionary of Engineering.* 2d ed. New York: McGraw-Hill Professional, 2003.

Tobin, James. *Great Projects: The Epic Story of Building America: From the Taming of the Mississippi to the Invention of the Internet.* New York: The Free Press, 2001.

Engineering technicians need mathematical and mechanical aptitude. They must understand abstract concepts and apply scientific principles to problems in the shop, laboratory, or work site.

Many tasks assigned to engineering technicians require patience and methodical, persistent work. Good technicians work well with their hands, paying close attention to every detail of a project. Some technicians are bored by the repetitiveness of some tasks, while others enjoy the routine.

Individuals planning to advance beyond the technician level should be willing to pursue some form of higher education.

EXPLORING

If you are interested in a career as an engineering technician, you can gain relevant experience by taking shop courses, joining electronics or radio clubs in school, and assembling electronic equipment with commercial kits.

You should take every opportunity to discuss the field with people working in it. Try to visit a variety of different kinds of engineering facilities—service shops, manufacturing plants, and research laboratories—either through individual visits or through field trips organized by teachers or guidance counselors. These visits will provide a realistic idea of the opportunities in the different areas of the industry. If you enroll in a community college or technical school, you may be able to secure off-quarter or part-time internships with local employers through your school's career services office. Internships are valuable ways to gain experience while still in school.

EMPLOYERS

Approximately 497,000 engineering technicians are employed in the United States. About 34 percent of all technicians work in manufacturing and 25 percent work in professional, scientific, and technical service industries.

STARTING OUT

Most technical schools, community colleges, and universities have career services offices. Companies actively recruit employees while they are still in school or are nearing graduation. Because these job services are the primary source of entry-level jobs for engineering technicians, you should check out a school's placement rate for your specific field before making a final decision about attending.

Another way to obtain employment is through direct contact with a particular company. It is best to write to the personnel department and include a resume summarizing your education and experience. If the company has an appropriate opening, a company representative will schedule an interview with you. There are also many excellent public and commercial employment organizations that can help graduates obtain jobs appropriate to their training and experience.

Newspaper want ads and employment services are other methods of getting jobs. Professional or trade magazines often have job listings and can be good sources for job seekers. Professional associations compile information on job openings and publish job lists. For example, the International Society of Certified Electronics Technicians offers lists of job openings around the country at its Web site. Information about job openings can also be found in trade magazines. Professional organizations are also good for networking with other technicians and are up to date on industry advancement, changes, and areas of employment.

ADVANCEMENT

As engineering technicians remain with a company, they become more valuable to their employer. Opportunities for advancement are available for engineering technicians who are willing to accept greater responsibilities either by specializing in a specific field, taking on more technically complex assignments, or by assuming supervisory duties. Some technicians advance by moving into technical sales or customer relations. Others pursue advanced education to become engineering technologists or engineers.

EARNINGS

The earnings of engineering technicians vary widely depending on their skills and experience, the type of work, geographical location, and other factors. The U.S. Department of Labor reports the following mean earnings for engineering technicians by specialty in 2008: aerospace engineering, $56,280; civil engineering, $45,730; electrical and electronics engineering, $53,990; environmental engineering, $44,440; industrial engineering, $50,070; and mechanical engineering, $50,040. Salaries ranged from less than $26,000 to $80,000 or more annually.

Engineering technicians generally receive premium pay for overtime work on Sundays and holidays and for evening and night-shift work. Most employers offer benefits packages that include paid holidays, paid vacations, sick days, and health insurance. Companies may also offer pension and retirement plans, profit sharing, 401(k) plans, tuition assistance programs, and release time for additional education.

WORK ENVIRONMENT

Depending on their jobs, engineering technicians may work in the shop or office areas or in both. The type of plant facilities depends on the product. For example, an electronics plant producing small electronic products requiring very exacting tolerances has very clean working conditions. Other engineering technicians, such as those in civil engineering, may work outdoors.

Engineering technicians often travel to other locations or areas. They may accompany engineers to technical conventions or on visits to other companies to gain insight into new or different methods of operation and production.

Continuing education plays a large role in the life of engineering technicians. They may attend classes or seminars, keeping up-to-date with emerging technology and methods of managing production efficiently.

Hours of work may vary and depend on factory shifts. Engineering technicians are often asked to get jobs done quickly and to meet very tight deadlines.

OUTLOOK

According to the *Occupational Outlook Handbook*, overall employment of engineering technicians is expected to increase more slowly than average for all occupations through 2018. Computer-aided design allows individual technicians to increase productivity, thereby limiting job growth. Those with training in sophisticated technologies and those with degrees in technology will have the best employment opportunities. Much faster than average employment growth is predicted for environmental engineering technicians as a result of increasing focus on the protection of the environment.

FOR MORE INFORMATION

Visit the society's precollege Web site for information on engineering and engineering technology careers.

American Society for Engineering Education
1818 N Street, NW, Suite 600
Washington, DC 20036-2479
Tel: 202-331-3500
http://www.engineeringk12.org/students/default.php

Contact the society for information on training and certification bodies.

American Society of Certified Engineering Technicians
PO Box 1536
Brandon, MS 39043-1536
Tel: 601-824-8991
http://www.ascet.org

This organization offers information on certification and student membership.

Electronics Technicians Association International
Five Depot Street
Greencastle, IN 46135-8024
Tel: 800-288-3824
Email: eta@eta-i.org
http://www.eta-i.org

Contact the society for information on certification and student membership.

International Society of Certified Electronics Technicians
3608 Pershing Avenue
Fort Worth, TX 76107-4527
Tel: 800-946-0201
Email: info@iscet.org
http://www.iscet.org

For information on careers, educational programs, and student clubs, contact

Junior Engineering Technical Society
1420 King Street, Suite 405
Alexandria, VA 22314-2750
Tel: 703-548-5387
Email: info@jets.org
http://www.jets.org

For information on certification, contact
National Institute for Certification in Engineering Technologies
1420 King Street, Suite 405
Alexandria, VA 22314-2750
Tel: 888-IS-NICET
http://www.nicet.org

Environmental Technicians

OVERVIEW

Environmental technicians, also known as *pollution control technicians,* conduct tests and field investigations to obtain soil samples and other data. Their research is used by engineers, scientists, and others who help clean up, monitor, control, or prevent pollution. An environmental technician usually specializes in air, water, or soil pollution. Although work differs by employer and specialty, technicians generally collect samples for laboratory analysis with specialized instruments and equipment; monitor pollution control devices and systems, such as smokestack air "scrubbers"; and perform various other tests and investigations to evaluate pollution problems. They follow strict procedures in collecting and recording data in order to meet the requirements of environmental laws.

In general, environmental technicians do not operate the equipment and systems designed to prevent pollution or remove pollutants. Instead, they test environmental conditions. In addition, some analyze and report on their findings.

There are approximately 35,000 environmental science and protection technicians, including health technicians, in the United States.

QUICK FACTS

School Subjects
Biology
Chemistry

Personal Skills
Mechanical/manipulative
Technical/scientific

Work Environment
Indoors and outdoors
One location with some
  travel

Minimum Education Level
Some postsecondary training

Salary Range
$25,830 to $40,230 to
  $70,000+

Certification or Licensing
Required for certain
  positions

Outlook
Much faster than the average

DOT
029

GOE
02.05.02

NOC
2231

O*NET-SOC
19-2041.00, 19-4091.00

HISTORY

Stricter pollution control regulations of the mid-1960s to early 1970s created a job market for environmental technicians. As regulations on industry have become more stringent, the job has grown both in importance and in scope. For centuries, the biosphere (the self-regulating "envelope" of air, water, and land in which all life on earth exists) was generally able to scatter, break down, or adapt to all the wastes and pollution produced by people.

This began to change drastically with the industrial revolution. Beginning in England in the 1750s, the industrial revolution caused the shift from a farming society to an industrialized society. Although it had many economic benefits, industrialization took a terrible toll on the environment. Textile manufacturing and iron processing spread through England, and coal-powered mills, machines, and factories spewed heavy black smoke into the air. Rivers and lakes became open sewers as factories dumped their wastes. By the 19th century, areas with high population density and clusters of factories were experiencing markedly higher death and disease rates than areas with little industrial development.

The industrial revolution spread all over the world, including France in the 1830s; Germany in the 1850s; the United States after the Civil War; and Russia and Asia (especially Japan) at the turn of the century. Wherever industry took hold, there were warning signs that the biosphere could not handle the resulting pollution. Smoke and smog hung over large cities from their many factories. Residents experienced more respiratory and other health problems. Manufacturing wastes and untreated sewage poisoned surface waters and underground sources of water, affecting water supplies and increasing disease. Wastes and pollution also seeped into the soil, affecting crops.

After World War II, the development of new synthetic materials and their resulting waste products, including plastics, pesticides, and vehicle exhaust that are difficult to degrade (break down), worsened pollution problems. Fish and wildlife began to die because rivers and lakes were choked with chemicals and wastes. Scientists documented connections between pollution and birth defects, cancer, fertility problems, genetic damage, and many other serious problems.

Not until the mid-1960s to early 1970s did public outcry, environmental activism, and political and economic necessity force the passage of stricter pollution control laws. Federal environmental legislation mandated cleanups of existing air, water, and soil pollution, and began to limit the type and amount of polluting substances that industry could release into the environment. Manufacturers were required to operate within stricter guidelines for air emissions, wastewater treatment and disposal, and other polluting activities. States and municipalities also were given increasing responsibilities for monitoring and working to reduce levels of auto, industrial, and other pollution. Out of the need to meet these new requirements, the pollution control industry was born—and with it, the job of environmental technician.

THE JOB

Environmental technicians usually specialize in one aspect of pollution control, such as water pollution, air pollution, or soil pollution. Sampling, monitoring, and testing are the major activities of the job. No matter what the specialty, environmental technicians work largely for or with government agencies that regulate pollution by industry.

Increasingly, technicians input their data into computers. Instruments used to collect water samples or monitor water sources may be highly sophisticated electronic devices. Technicians usually do not analyze the data they collect. However, they may report on what they know to scientists or engineers, either verbally or in writing.

The following paragraphs detail specialties in the field:

Water pollution technicians monitor both industrial and residential discharge, such as from wastewater treatment plants. They help to determine the presence and extent of pollutants in water. They collect samples from lakes, streams, rivers, groundwater (the water under the earth), industrial or municipal wastewater, or other sources. Samples are brought to labs, where chemical and other tests are performed. If the samples contain harmful substances, remedial (cleanup) actions will need to be taken. These technicians also may perform various field tests, such as checking the pH, oxygen, and nitrate level of surface waters.

Some water pollution technicians set up monitoring equipment to obtain information on water flow, movement, temperature, or pressure and record readings from these devices. To trace flow patterns, they may inject dyes into the water.

Technicians have to be careful not to contaminate their samples, stray from the specific testing procedure, or otherwise do something to ruin the sample or cause faulty or misleading results.

Depending on the specific job, water pollution technicians may spend a good part of their time outdoors, in good weather and bad, aboard boats, and sometimes near unpleasant smells or potentially hazardous substances. Field sites may be in remote areas. In some cases, the technician may have to fly to a different part of the country, perhaps staying away from home for a long period of time.

Water pollution technicians play a big role in industrial wastewater discharge monitoring, treatment, and control. Nearly every manufacturing process produces wastewater, but U.S. manufacturers today are required to be more careful about what they discharge with their wastewater.

Some technicians specialize in groundwater, ocean water, or other types of natural waters. *Estuarine resource technicians,* for example, specialize in estuary waters, or coastal areas where fresh water and salt water come together. These bays, salt marshes, inlets, and other tidal water bodies support a wide variety of plant and animal life with ecologically complex relationships. They are vulnerable to destructive pollution from adjoining industries, cities and towns, and other sources. Estuarine resource technicians aid scientists in studying the resulting environmental changes. They may work in laboratories or aboard boats, or may use diving gear to collect samples directly.

Air pollution technicians collect and test air samples (for example, from chimneys of industrial manufacturing plants), record data on atmospheric conditions (such as determining levels of airborne substances from auto or industrial emissions), and supply data to scientists and engineers for further testing and analysis. In labs, air pollution technicians may help test air samples or re-create contaminants. They may use atomic absorption spectrophotometers, flame photometers, gas chromatographs, and other instruments for analyzing samples.

In the field, air pollution technicians may use rooftop sampling devices or operate mobile monitoring units or stationary trailers. The trailers may be equipped with elaborate automatic testing systems, including some of the same devices found in laboratories. Outside air is pumped into various chambers in the trailer where it is analyzed for the presence of pollutants. The results can be recorded by machine on 30-day rolls of graph paper or fed into a computer at regular intervals. Technicians set up and maintain the sampling devices, replenish the chemicals used in tests, replace worn parts, calibrate instruments, and record results. Some air pollution technicians specialize in certain pollutants or pollution sources. For example, *engine emission technicians* focus on exhaust from internal combustion engines.

Soil or *land pollution technicians* collect soil, silt, or mud samples and check them for contamination. Soil can become contaminated when polluted water seeps into the earth, such as when liquid waste leaks from a landfill or other source into surrounding ground. Soil pollution technicians work for federal, state, and local government agencies, for private consulting firms, and elsewhere. (Some soil conservation technicians perform pollution control work.)

A position sometimes grouped with other environmental technicians is that of *noise pollution technician*. Noise pollution technicians use rooftop devices and mobile units to take readings and collect data on noise levels of factories, highways, airports, and other locations in order to determine noise exposure levels for workers or the public. Some test noise levels of construction equipment, chain saws, snow blowers, lawn mowers, or other equipment.

REQUIREMENTS

High School

In high school, key courses include biology, chemistry, and physics. Conservation or ecology courses also will be useful, if offered at your school. Math classes should include at least algebra and geometry, and taking English and speech classes will help to sharpen your communication skills. In addition, work on developing your computer skills while in high school, either on your own or through a class.

Postsecondary Training

Some technician positions call for a high school diploma plus employer training. As environmental work becomes more technical and complex, more positions are being filled by technicians with at least an associate's degree. To meet this need, many community colleges across the country have developed appropriate programs for environmental technicians. Areas of study include environmental engineering technologies, pollution control technologies, conservation, and ecology. Courses include meteorology, toxicology, source testing, sampling, and analysis, air quality management, environmental science, and statistics. Other training requirements vary by employer. Some experts advise attending school in the part of the country where you'd like to begin your career so you can start getting to know local employers before you graduate.

Certification or Licensing

Certification or licensing is required for some positions in pollution control, especially those in which sanitation, public health, a public water supply, or a sewage treatment system is involved. For example, the Institute of Professional Environmental Practice offers the qualified environmental professional and the environmental professional intern certifications. See the end of this article for contact information.

What You Can Do to Prevent Air Pollution

Approximately 42 percent of the U.S. population lives in counties that have unhealthful levels of either particle pollution or ozone (a highly reactive gas that can be harmful to humans), according to the American Lung Association's *State of the Air: 2008*. This may seem like a daunting problem, but there are things you can do to help reduce air pollution. The American Lung Association offers the following tips:

- Drive Less. Reduce vehicle emissions by combining errands, taking public transportation, walking, bicycling, and encourage your community to build more pedestrian- and public-transportation-friendly infrastructure.

- Get Involved. Support local and state government attempts to reduce air pollution.

- Avoid Burning Trash or Wood. Burning these materials creates large amounts of particulates—a major source of pollution.

- Reduce Your Use of Electricity. Electricity generation is a major cause of pollution.

Other Requirements

Environmental technicians should be curious, patient, detail-oriented, and capable of following instructions. Basic manual skills are a must for collecting samples and performing similar tasks. Complex environmental regulations drive technicians' jobs; therefore, it's crucial that they are able to read and understand technical materials and to carefully follow any written guidelines for sampling or other procedures. Computer skills and the ability to read and interpret maps, charts, and diagrams are also necessary.

Technicians must make accurate and objective observations, maintain clear and complete records, and be exact in their computations. In addition, good physical conditioning is a requirement for some activities, for example, climbing up smokestacks to take emission samples.

EXPLORING

To learn more about environmental jobs, visit your local library and read some technical and general-interest environmental science publications. This might give you an idea of the technologies being used and issues being discussed in the field today. You also can visit a municipal health department or pollution control agency in your community. Many agencies are pleased to explain their work to visitors.

School science clubs, local community groups, and naturalist clubs may help broaden your understanding of various aspects of the natural world and give you some experience. Most schools have recycling programs that enlist student help.

With the help of a teacher or career counselor, a tour of a local manufacturing plant using an air- or water-pollution abatement system also might be arranged. Many plants offer tours of their operations to the public. This may provide an excellent opportunity to see technicians at work.

As a high school student, it may be difficult to obtain summer or part-time work as a technician due to the extensive operations and safety training required for some of these jobs. However, it is worthwhile to check with a local environmental agency, nonprofit environmental organizations, or private consulting firms to learn of volunteer or paid support opportunities. Any hands-on experience you can get will be of value to a future employer.

EMPLOYERS

Approximately 35,000 environmental science and protection technicians are employed in the United States. Many jobs for environmental technicians are with the government agencies that monitor the environment, such as the Environmental Protection Agency (EPA), and the U.S. Departments of Agriculture, Energy, and Interior.

Water pollution technicians may be employed by manufacturers that produce wastewater, municipal wastewater treatment facilities, private firms hired to monitor or control pollutants in water or wastewater, and government regulatory agencies responsible for protecting water quality.

Air pollution technicians work for government agencies such as regional EPA offices. They also work for private manufacturers producing airborne pollutants, research facilities, pollution control equipment manufacturers, and other employers.

Soil pollution technicians may work for federal or state departments of agriculture and EPA offices. They also work for private agricultural groups that monitor soil quality for pesticide levels.

Noise pollution technicians are employed by private companies and by government agencies such as OSHA (Occupational Safety and Health Administration).

STARTING OUT

Graduates of two-year environmental programs are often employed during their final term by recruiters who visit their schools. Specific opportunities will vary depending on the part of the country, the segment of the environmental industry, the specialization of the technician (air, water, or land), the economy, and other factors. Many beginning technicians find the greatest number of positions available in state or local government agencies.

Most schools provide job-hunting advice and assistance. Direct application to state or local environmental agencies, employment agencies, or potential employers can also be a productive approach. If you hope to find employment outside your current geographic area, you may get good results by checking with professional organizations or by reading advertisements in technical journals, many of which have searchable job listings on the Internet.

ADVANCEMENT

The typical hierarchy for environmental work is technician (two years of postsecondary education or less), technologist (two years or more of postsecondary training), technician manager (perhaps a technician or technologist with many years of experience), and scientist or engineer (four-year bachelor of science degree or more, up to Ph.D. level).

In some private manufacturing or consulting firms, technician positions are used for training newly recruited professional staff. In such cases, workers with four-year degrees in engineering or physical science are likely to be promoted before those with two-year degrees. Employees of government agencies usually are organized under civil service systems that specify experience, education, and other criteria for advancement. Private industry promotions are structured differently and will depend on a variety of factors.

EARNINGS

Pay for environmental technicians varies widely depending on the nature of the work they do, training and experience required for the work, type of employer, geographic region, and other factors. Public-sector positions tend to pay less than private-sector positions.

According to the U.S. Department of Labor, the average annual salary for environmental science and protection technicians was

$40,230 in 2008. Salaries ranged from less than $25,830 to more than $64,580. Technicians who worked for local government earned mean annual salaries of $47,100 in 2008; those who were employed by state government earned $47,190. Technicians who become managers or supervisors can earn $70,000 per year or more. Technicians who work in private industry or who further their education to secure teaching positions can also expect to earn higher than average salaries.

No matter which area they specialize in, environmental technicians generally enjoy fringe benefits such as paid vacation, holidays and sick time, and employer-paid training. Technicians who work full time (and some who work part time) often receive health insurance benefits. Technicians who are employed by the federal government may get additional benefits, such as pension and retirement benefits.

WORK ENVIRONMENT

Conditions range from clean and pleasant indoor offices and laboratories to hot, cold, wet, bad-smelling, noisy, or even hazardous settings outdoors. Anyone planning a career in environmental technology should realize the possibility of exposure to unpleasant or unsafe conditions at least occasionally in his or her career. Employers often can minimize these negatives through special equipment and procedures. Most laboratories and manufacturing companies have safety procedures for potentially dangerous situations.

Some jobs involve vigorous physical activity, such as handling a small boat or climbing a tall ladder. For the most part, technicians need only to be prepared for moderate activity. Travel may be required; technicians go to urban, industrial, or rural settings for sampling.

Because their job can involve a considerable amount of repetitive work, patience and the ability to handle routine are important. Yet, particularly when environmental technicians are working in the field, they also have to be ready to use their resourcefulness and ingenuity to find the best ways of responding to new situations.

OUTLOOK

Demand for environmental technicians is expected to increase much faster than the average for all occupations through 2018, according to the U.S. Department of Labor. Those trained to handle increasingly complex technical demands will have the best employment prospects. Environmental technicians will be needed to collect soil, water, and air samples to measure the levels of pollutants; to monitor the private industry's compliance with environmental regulations; and to clean up contaminated sites. Most employment growth will occur in professional, scientific, and technical services.

Demand will be higher in some areas of the country than others depending on specialty; for example, air pollution technicians will be especially in demand in large cities, such as Los Angeles and New York, which face pressure to comply with national air quality standards. Amount of industrialization, stringency of state and local pollution control enforcement, health of local economy, and other factors also will affect demand by region and specialty. Perhaps the greatest factors affecting environmental work are continued mandates for pollution control by the federal government. As long as the federal government supports pollution control, environmental technicians will be needed.

FOR MORE INFORMATION

For information on environmental careers and degree programs, contact
Advanced Technology Environmental and Energy Center
500 Belmont Road
Bettendorf, IA 52722-5649
http://www.ateec.org

For job listings and certification information, contact
Air & Waste Management Association
420 Fort Duquesne Boulevard
One Gateway Center, 3rd Floor
Pittsburgh, PA 15222-1435
Tel: 412-232-3444
Email: info@awma.org
http://www.awma.org

For information on the engineering field and technician certification, contact
American Society of Certified Engineering Technicians
PO Box 1536
Brandon, MS 39043-1536
Tel: 601-824-8991
http://www.ascet.org

For information on certification, contact
Institute of Professional Environmental Practice
600 Forbes Avenue
339 Fisher Hall
Pittsburgh, PA 15282-0001
Tel: 412-396-1703
Email: ipep@duq.edu
http://www.ipep.org

For job listings and scholarship opportunities, contact
National Ground Water Association
601 Dempsey Road
Westerville, OH 43081-8978
Tel: 800-551-7379
Email: ngwa@ngwa.org
http://www.ngwa.org

For information on environmental careers and student employment opportunities, contact
U.S. Environmental Protection Agency
Ariel Rios Building
1200 Pennsylvania Avenue, NW
Washington, DC 20460-0001
Tel: 202-272-0167
http://www.epa.gov

For information on conferences and workshops, contact
Water Environment Federation
601 Wythe Street
Alexandria, VA 22314-1994
Tel: 800-666-0206
http://www.wef.org

Fiber Optics Technicians

QUICK FACTS

School Subjects
Mathematics
Technical/shop

Personal Skills
Mechanical/manipulative
Technical/scientific

Work Environment
Indoors and outdoors
Primarily multiple locations

Minimum Education Level
High school diploma

Salary Range
$25,790 to $48,090 to
$67,990+

Certification or Licensing
Voluntary

Outlook
Little or no change

DOT
N/A

GOE
05.02.01

NOC
7246

O*NET-SOC
49-9052.00

OVERVIEW

Fiber optics technicians work with the optical fibers and cables used in transmitting communications data. Depending on the area of employment, technicians splice fibers, fuse fibers together, and install fiber cables beneath ground and in buildings. These technicians work for telephone and cable companies and other businesses involved in telecommunications.

HISTORY

A need to convey messages quickly led to experimentation in the use of light to communicate. Before the introduction of the electric telegraph in the mid-1800s, a series of semaphores (systems if visual signaling) atop towers allowed for communication between tower operators. Ships also used light signals to communicate with each other. But the reliability of wires to carry electricity, and the invention of the electric telegraph and the telephone, put the further development of optical communications on hold.

Studies in the field of medicine led to the discovery that rods of glass or plastic could carry light. In the 1950s these developments helped such engineers as Alec Reeves of Great Britain in the experimentation of fiber optics for telecommunications. Increasing television and telephone use demanded more transmission bandwidth, and the invention of the laser in 1960 made optical communications a reality. Technical barriers remained, however, and experimentation continued for many years, leading to the first telephone field trials in 1977. Today,

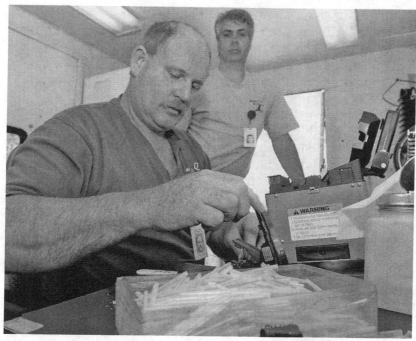

Technicians splice fiber optic cable for a new installation at an office. *(Ed Andrieski, AP Photo)*

the career of fiber optics technician is instrumental to communications, as telecommunications companies recognize the importance of fiber optics in the future of high-speed, high-definition phone and Internet service, the majority of which is now transmitted by fiber optics.

THE JOB

Fiber optics technicians prepare, install, and test fiber optics transmission systems. These systems are composed of fiber optic cables and allow for data communication between computers, phones, and faxes. When working for a telecommunications company, fiber optics technicians are often required to install lines for local area networks; these data networks serve small areas of linked computers, such as in an office.

The telecommunications company for which a technician works will contract with a company to create a communications system. A sales worker will evaluate the customer's needs and then order the materials for the installation. Fiber optics technicians take these materials to the job site. Each job site may be very different—technicians may work in a variety of different locales. First, fiber optics technicians need to get a sense of the area. They walk through with the client, evaluating the areas where they will install fiber optic cable. Newer buildings will be readily equipped for installation; in some older buildings, it may be more difficult to get behind ceiling tiles and in the walls.

After they have readied the area for cable, fiber optics technicians run the cable from the computer's mainframe to individual workstations. They then test the cable, using power meters and other devices, by running a laser through it. Fiber optics technicians use equipment that measures the amount of time it takes for the laser to go through, determining any signal loss or faults in the fiber link.

Technicians may also fuse fibers together. This involves cleaning the fiber and cutting it with a special diamond-headed cleaver. After they have prepared both ends, they place them into a fusion splicer. At the press of a button, the splicer fuses the two fibers together.

REQUIREMENTS

High School

There are not really any specific high school courses that will prepare you specifically for work as a fiber optics technician, but many courses provide relevant skills. Shop classes will give you experience working with tools to complete a variety of projects; speech and writing classes will help you improve your communication skills; and mathematics classes will prepare you to work with computations and installation plans.

Postsecondary Training

A college degree is not required but can give you an edge when looking for work as a fiber optics technician. A number of community colleges across the country offer programs in fiber optics technology or broadband networks technology. (Visit http://www.thefoa.org/foa_aprv.htm for a list of programs that have been approved by the Fiber Optic Association.) These programs offer such courses as cable construction, fiber optic installation techniques, singlemode and multimode systems, and wavelength and bandwidth. They also may include lab and certification components. Short-term training opportunities, lasting only a few days, may also be available at some schools.

Certification or Licensing

The Fiber Optic Association offers the following voluntary certifications: certified fiber optic technician, certified fiber optic technician for FTTx (fiber to the home, fiber to the premises, fiber to the curb), certified premises cabling technician, advanced fiber optic technician, certified fiber optic specialist, and certified fiber optic instructor. The Electronics Technicians Association International offers several certifications in fiber optics. The Telecommunications Industry Association offers a certification program for technicians working in convergence technologies, and the International Association for Radio, Telecommunications and Electromagnetics offers certification for technicians employed in the telecommunications industry. Additionally, ACES International provides certification for fiber optics technicians.

Other Requirements

Because of the fine nature of the fibers, you should have a steady hand and good eyesight in assembling fiber optic cables. You will also need good math skills for working with detailed plans and designs. Some companies may require you to have your own special fiber optic tools.

EXPLORING

Visit the Web sites of the associations listed at the end of this article to learn more about the industry. Ask a teacher to set up an interview with an experienced fiber optics technician. Talking with someone in the field is the best way to learn the pros and cons of any career.

EMPLOYERS

Fiber optics technicians work for telephone companies, cable companies, and computer networking businesses. They may also work as freelancers, hiring on with companies on special installation projects.

STARTING OUT

There are many sources of information about developments in fiber optics and the telecommunications industry, including professional associations and Web sites. When you complete a fiber optics technology program, your school will be able to direct you to local job opportunities. Information Gatekeepers publishes the *Optical Networks/Fiber Optics Yellow Pages*, a directory that lists more than 1,000 companies. For more information, visit Information Gatekeepers' Web site, http://www.igigroup.com.

Earnings for Telecommunications Line Installers and Repairers by Industry, 2008

Field	Mean Annual Earnings
Satellite telecommunications	$58,830
Wired telecommunications carriers	$51,560
Telecommunications resellers	$58,100
Building equipment contractors	$40,410
Cable and other subscription programming	$42,560
Cable and other program distribution	$39,970
Utility system construction	$36,430

Source: U.S. Department of Labor

ADVANCEMENT

Even without special fiber optics training, fiber optics technicians may be able to enter the job market in an entry-level position with a telecommunications company. The company may have its own training program, or offer tuition reimbursement for outside seminars in fiber optics technology. After they've gained experience working with fiber optic cable, fiber optics technicians may be able to move into a management or executive position. They may also become consultants, advising companies on data transmission problems.

EARNINGS

The U.S. Department of Labor reports the following median hourly earnings for telecommunications line installers and repairers (which include those who work with fiber optics) by employer in 2008: satellite communications, $58,800; wired telecommunications carriers, $51,560; telecommunications resellers, $58,100; cable and other subscription programming, $42,560; and cable and other program distribution, $39,970. Salaries for all line installers and repairers ranged from less than $25,790 to $67,990 or more per year.

Companies offer a variety of benefit packages, which can include any of the following: paid holidays, vacations, and sick days; personal days; medical, dental, and life insurance; profit-sharing plans; 401(k) plans; retirement and pension plans; and educational assistance programs.

WORK ENVIRONMENT

Fiber optics technicians who work as assemblers spend most of their time sitting at a bench. Technicians who work as installers usually work out in the field installing fiber beneath the ground. There is little physical exertion required because machinery is used to dig the trenches. Fiber optics technicians spend part of their time outside repairing fiber, and part of their time in a van preparing the fibers for installation. They may also install fiber cables in buildings; this will require some climbing of ladders and working beneath floorboards.

OUTLOOK

The U.S. Department of Labor projects that employment of telecommunications line installers and repairers will experience little or no change through 2018. The growth of wireless and satellite communications technologies for use in the delivery of communications, video, and data services will limit job growth in the field.

Digital transmissions will soon be the norm for telecommunications—not only do modern offices require data communications systems, but cable companies are investing in fiber optics to offer digital TV and cable, as well as quality phone service. Also, the cost of fiber is dropping, which means more companies will invest in fiber optics. As a result, experienced fiber optics assemblers and installers will find job opportunities. Additionally, strong employment opportunities should be available for fiber optics technicians who work for telephone companies connecting fiber from exterior lines to customers' homes or business. The Fiber Optic Association reports that major phone companies are "committing billions of dollars to plans for connecting millions of homes and offices with fiber in the future."

FOR MORE INFORMATION

For certification information, contact
ACES International
5381 Chatham Lake Drive
Virginia Beach, VA 23464-5400
Tel: 757-499-2850

Email: aces@acesinternational.org
http://www.acesinternational.org

For information on certification, contact
Electronics Technicians Association International
Five Depot Street
Greencastle, IN 46135-8024
Tel: 800-288-3824
Email: eta@eta-i.org
http://www.eta-i.org

For information on optics and careers in the field, visit
Exploring the Science of Light!
http://www.opticsforteens.org

To learn about certification and approved training programs, contact
Fiber Optic Association
1119 South Mission Road, #355
Fallbrook, CA 92028-3225
Tel: 760-451-3655
Email: info@thefoa.org
http://www.thefoa.org

For information on certification, contact
**International Association for Radio, Telecommunications and
    Electromagnetics**
840 Queen Street
New Bern, NC 28560-4856
Tel: 800-89-NARTE
http://www.narte.org

*To learn about telecommunications technology and uses for fiber
optics, visit the society's Web site.*
Optical Society of America
2010 Massachusetts Avenue, NW
Washington, DC 20036-1012
Tel: 202-223-8130
http://www.osa.org

For information on educational training in optics, visit
Optics and Photonics Education Directory
http://www.opticseducation.org

For information on certification, contact
Telecommunications Industry Association
2500 Wilson Boulevard, Suite 300
Arlington, VA 22201-3834
Tel: 703-907-7700
http://www.tiaonline.org

To learn about opportunities for women in the fiber optics industry, contact
Women in Cable Telecommunications
14555 Avion Parkway, Suite 250
Chantilly, VA 20151-1117
Tel: 703-234-9810
http://www.wict.org

For career advice on issues such as networking, interviewing, and job searching in the field of optics, visit the following Web site organized by the Optical Society of America:
Work in Optics
http://www.workinoptics.com

Fluid Power Technicians

QUICK FACTS

School Subjects
Mathematics
Technical/shop

Personal Skills
Mechanical/manipulative
Technical/scientific

Work Environment
Primarily indoors
Primarily multiple locations

Minimum Education Level
Some postsecondary training

Salary Range
$30,794 to $40,569 to
$51,065+

Certification or Licensing
Voluntary

Outlook
Faster than the average

DOT
600

GOE
08.02.03

NOC
2132

O*NET-SOC
N/A

OVERVIEW

Fluid power technicians, also known as *hydraulic and pneumatic power technicians,* work with equipment that utilizes the pressure of a liquid or gas in a closed container to transmit, multiply, or control power. Working under the supervision of an engineer or engineering staff, they assemble, install, maintain, and test fluid power equipment, which is found in almost every facet of daily life in the United States.

HISTORY

Machinery that is operated by using fluid power has been in use for thousands of years. In Roman times, water flowing past a rotating paddle wheel produced power for milling. Early leather bellows, hand-operated by blacksmiths, were the first known devices to use compressed air. In Italy, in the 16th century, a more sophisticated bellows was invented that used falling water to compress air. Shortly thereafter, Denis Papin, a French physicist, used power from a waterwheel to compress air in a similar manner.

The 19th century brought the first practical application of an air-driven, piston-operated hammer, invented in Great Britain by George Law. In the mid-1800s, water-cooled reciprocating compressors were introduced in the United States and resulted in the development of large compressed-air units that factory workers used to operate industrial tools. In 1875 American engineer and industrialist George Westinghouse created and utilized a continuous automatic compressed-air brake system for trains.

In the latter part of the 19th century and the early part of the 20th, experiments in fluid dynamics by Osborne Reynolds and Ludwig Prandtl led to a new understanding of the way fluid behaves in certain circumstances. These findings laid the groundwork for modern fluid power mechanics. The 20th and 21st centuries have witnessed a significant increase in the use of fluid power for many different applications.

Fluid power workers are now employed in any number of industries, from aerospace to materials handling. Fluid power is also routinely used and depended upon in daily life. Anyone who has ever ridden in a car, for example, has relied upon fluid power to operate its hydraulic braking system. With fluid power so widely used, many businesses throughout the United States employ men and women who are trained in its various aspects. Fluid power technicians, with their specialized skills and knowledge, have become a mainstay of industrial support groups that work with this type of machinery.

THE JOB

Many different machines use some kind of fluid power system, including agricultural, manufacturing, defense, and mining equipment. We come across fluid power systems every day when we use automatic door closers, bicycle pumps, and spray guns. Even automobile transmissions incorporate fluid power.

There are two types of fluid power machines. The first kind—hydraulic machines—use water, oil, or another liquid in a closed system to transmit the energy needed to do work. For example, a hydraulic jack, which can be used to lift heavy loads, is a cylinder with a piston fitted inside it. When a liquid is pumped into the bottom of the cylinder, the piston is forced upward, lifting the weight on the jack. To lower the weight, the liquid is released through a valve, returning the pressure in the system to normal.

Pneumatic machines, the other type of fluid power systems, are activated by the pressure of air or another gas in a closed system. Pavement-breaking jackhammers and compressed-air paint sprayers are common examples of pneumatic machines.

Fluid power systems are a part of most machines used in industry, so fluid power technicians work in many different settings. Most often, however, they work in factories where fluid power systems are used in manufacturing. In such a factory, for example, they might maintain and service pneumatic machines that bolt together products on an automated assembly line.

In their work, fluid power technicians analyze blueprints, drawings, and specifications; set up various milling, shaping, grinding, and drilling machines; make precision parts; use sensitive measuring instruments to make sure the parts are exactly the required size; and use hand and power tools to put together components of the fluid power system they are assembling or repairing.

Technicians may also be responsible for testing fluid power systems. To determine whether a piece of equipment is working properly, they connect the unit to test equipment that measures such factors as fluid pressure, flow rates, and power loss from friction or wear. Based on their analysis of the test results, they may advise changes in the equipment setup or instrumentation.

Some technicians work for companies that research better ways to develop and use fluid power systems. They may work in laboratories as part of research and development teams that set up fluid power equipment and test it under operating conditions. Other technicians work as sales and service representatives for companies that make and sell fluid power equipment to industrial plants. These technicians travel from one plant to another, providing customers with specialized information and assistance with their equipment. Some technicians repair and maintain fluid power components of heavy equipment used in construction, on farms, or in mining. Because fluid power technology is important in the flight controls, landing gear, and brakes of airplanes, many technicians are also employed in the aircraft industry.

REQUIREMENTS

High School
If you are considering a career in fluid power, you should take as many courses as possible in computer science and mathematics. Physics, shop, drafting, and English will also provide a solid background for this type of work.

Postsecondary Training
In the past, you could become a fluid power technician with only a high school diploma and, perhaps, some related technical experience. Technicians were trained in fluid power technology by their employers or by taking short courses or workshops. Today, however, most employers prefer to hire fluid power technicians who have at least two years of post-high school training, such as that offered by community and technical colleges.

There are fewer than 40 technical training programs in the United States that focus primarily on fluid power technology. A student enrolled in one of these programs might expect to take classes on very specialized topics, such as fluid power math, process and fabrication fundamentals, hydraulic components and accessories, pneumatic components and circuits, and advanced systems calculations. If it is not possible to attend one of the schools that offer programs in fluid power, training in a related field, such as mechanical or electrical technology, can provide adequate preparation for employment.

Certification or Licensing

Certification for fluid power technicians is voluntary. Offered through the Fluid Power Certification Board, the certification process is administered by the International Fluid Power Society. Applicants must pass a three-hour, written examination and a three-hour job performance test before receiving technician certification. This certification may be beneficial to technicians in finding jobs, obtaining more advanced positions, or receiving higher pay.

Other Requirements

Technicians must be able to understand and analyze mechanical systems. In order to do this well, you should have both mechanical aptitude and an analytical mindset. Because you will often work as a member of a team, an ability to work well and communicate easily with others is important. Finally, you should enjoy challenges and the process of troubleshooting problems.

EXPLORING

Your school or public library should have books that explain the field of fluid power. If you happen to live near one of the schools that offer a degree in fluid power technology, it may be possible to arrange a meeting with instructors or students in the program. Talking with a fluid power technician can be an excellent way of learning about the job firsthand. Finally, taking certain classes, such as machine shop, physics, or electronics, might help you gauge your enjoyment and ability level for this work.

EMPLOYERS

The largest consumers of fluid power products are the aerospace, construction equipment, agricultural equipment, machine tool, and material handling industries, according to the National Fluid Power Association. Fluid power also provides power for auxiliary systems on planes, ships, trains, and trucks.

STARTING OUT

Most fluid power technicians obtain their jobs through their community and technical college career services offices. In addition, organizations such as the International Fluid Power Society and the Fluid Power Educational Foundation have lists of their corporate members that can be used to start a job search. Some openings might be listed in the employment sections of newspapers.

ADVANCEMENT

Some technicians advance simply by becoming more knowledgeable and skilled in their work and eventually receive more responsibility. Another route for technicians is to become a fluid power specialist by taking additional training and upgrading their certification. A specialist designs and applies systems and can instruct newer employees on the basics of fluid power systems.

Some technicians go into sales and marketing, using their experience and knowledge to provide customers with technical assistance. Another option is to become a *fluid power consultant,* who works with different companies to analyze, design, or improve fluid power systems.

EARNINGS

Salaries for fluid power technicians vary according to geographic location and industry. According to CBsalary.com, beginning fluid power technicians can expect to earn around $30,794. The average salary for all fluid power technicians is $40,569, and the highest paid technicians can earn $51,065 or more. Those who move into consulting or other advanced positions can earn even more. Most workers in this field receive a full benefits package, often including vacation days, sick leave, medical and life insurance, and a retirement plan.

WORK ENVIRONMENT

Because fluid power technicians work in any number of different industries, their work environments vary. Many work in industrial settings and must spend much of their time on the manufacturing floor. In this case, they may have to become accustomed to noise and heat generated by the machinery, although the industry is addressing the noise-level issue. Others work in laboratories or testing facilities. Those involved in sales and marketing or in installing and repairing equipment may travel to different customer locations.

The work is frequently dirty, as technicians often have to handle machinery that has been used and may be leaking fluid. Also, working on large machinery and components requires physical strength and may require being in areas where safety regulations must be followed.

Many workers in this field find their jobs enjoyable and satisfying. Because they deal with different problems and solutions all the time, the work is challenging, interesting, and not repetitive. It can also be gratifying to figure out how to make a machine run properly or improve upon its performance through testing and experimenting.

OUTLOOK

Because fluid power is used in so many different industries, the need for technicians is growing rapidly. Currently, in fact, demand exceeds the supply of trained workers. In recent decades, electrohydraulic and electropneumatic technologies opened up new markets, such as active suspensions on automobiles, and reestablished older markets, such as robotics. Therefore, the fluid power industry is expected to continue growing and the outlook for technicians should remain strong through the next decade.

FOR MORE INFORMATION

For a list of schools offering courses in fluid power technology and information about scholarships, contact
Fluid Power Educational Foundation
PO Box 1420
Cherry Hill, NJ 08034-0054
Tel: 856-424-8998
Email: info@fpef.org
http://www.fpef.org

For industry information, contact
FPDA Motion & Control Network
105 Eastern Ave, Suite 104
Annapolis, MD 21403-3366
Tel: 410-263-1014
Email: info@fpda.org
http://www.fpda.org

For information on certification, contact
International Fluid Power Society
PO Box 1420
Cherry Hill, NJ 08034-0054
Tel: 800-308-6005
Email: info@ifps.org
http://www.ifps.org

For career information, a list of educational programs that offer training in fluid power technology, and an overview of the fluid power industry, contact
National Fluid Power Association
3333 North Mayfair Road, Suite 211
Milwaukee, WI 53222-3219
Tel: 414-778-3344
Email: nfpa@nfpa.com
http://www.nfpa.com

Instrumentation Technicians

QUICK FACTS

School Subjects
Mathematics
Physics
Technical/shop

Personal Skills
Mechanical/manipulative
Technical/scientific

Work Environment
Primarily indoors
Primarily one location

Minimum Education Level
Associate's degree

Salary Range
$25,580 to $48,110 to
$71,380+

Certification or Licensing
Voluntary

Outlook
About as fast as the average

DOT
003

GOE
05.01.01

NOC
2243

O*NET-SOC
17-3023.02, 17-3024.00,
17-3027.00, 49-9062.00,
49-9069.00

OVERVIEW

Instrumentation technicians are skilled craftsworkers who do precision work and are involved in the field of measurement and control. Technicians inspect, test, repair, and adjust instruments that detect, measure, and record changes in industrial environments. They work with theoretical or analytical problems, helping engineers improve instrument and system performance.

HISTORY

The use of instruments as a means for people to monitor and control their environment and to guide their activities is as old as the sundial. As modern technology progresses, we still find ourselves in need of precise information that is sometimes difficult for a person to physically obtain.

For instance, with the advent of the steam engine in the 19th century, a train operator had to know how much pressure was inside a boiler. A gauge was designed to measure this safely. The early 20th century saw the development of the internal combustion engine and powered flight. With these developments, engineers and technicians designed and made instruments such as speedometers, altimeters, and tachometers to provide vital data for the safe operation of these engines and auxiliary equipment.

Since World War II, instrumentation technology has become a fast-growing field, responding to challenging needs as people explore space, research our oceans, perform biomedical studies, and advance nuclear

94

technology. Today, instrumentation technology involves both measurement and control, and technicians are critical to their accurate operation. For instance, instrumentation technicians at nuclear reactors assure that the devices inside accurately measure heat, pressure, and radiation, and their rates of change. If any of these factors is not at its specific level, then other instruments make the necessary adjustments. This allows the plant to operate safely and efficiently.

THE JOB

Instrumentation technicians work with complex instruments that detect, measure, and record changes in industrial environments. As part of their duties, these technicians perform tests, develop new instruments, and install, repair, inspect, and maintain the instruments. Examples of such instruments include altimeters, pressure gauges, speedometers, and radiation detection devices.

Some instrumentation technicians operate the laboratory equipment that produces or records the effects of certain conditions on the test instruments, such as vibration, stress, temperature, humidity, pressure, altitude, and acceleration. Other technicians sketch, build, and modify electronic and mechanical fixtures, instruments, and related apparatuses.

As part of their duties, technicians might verify the dimensions and functions of devices assembled by other technicians and craftsworkers, plan test programs, and direct technical personnel in carrying out these tests. Instrumentation technicians also perform mathematical calculations on instrument readings and test results so they can be used in graphs and written reports.

Instrumentation technicians work with three major categories of instruments: 1) pneumatic and electropneumatic equipment, which includes temperature and flow transmitters and receivers and devices that start or are started by such things as pressure springs, diaphragms, and bellows; 2) hydraulic instrumentation, which includes hydraulic valves, hydraulic valve operators, and electrohydraulic equipment; and 3) electrical and electronic equipment, which includes electrical sensing elements and transducers and electronic and digital recorders and telemetering systems.

In some industries a technician might work on equipment from each category, while in others a technician might be responsible for only one specific type of task. The different levels of responsibility depend also on the instrumentation technician's level of training and experience.

Instrumentation technicians may hold a variety of different positions. *Mechanical instrumentation technicians,* for example, handle routine mechanical functions. They check out equipment before operation, calibrate it during operation, rebuild it using standard replacement parts, mount interconnecting equipment from blueprints, and perform routine repairs using common hand tools. They must be able to read both instrumentation and electronic schematic diagrams. *Instrumentation repair technicians* determine the causes of malfunctions and make repairs. Such repairs usually involve individual pieces of equipment, as distinguished from entire systems. This job requires experience, primarily laboratory-oriented, beyond that of mechanical instrumentation technicians.

Troubleshooting instrumentation technicians make adjustments to instruments and control systems, calibrate equipment, set up tests, diagnose malfunctions, and revise existing systems. They work either on-site or at a workbench. Advanced training in mathematics, physics, and graphics is required for this level of work. Technicians who are involved in the design of instruments are called *instrumentation design technicians*. They work under the supervision of a design engineer. Using information prepared by engineers, they build models and prototypes and prepare sketches, working drawings, and diagrams. These technicians also test out new system designs, order parts, and make mock-ups of new systems.

Technicians in certain industries have more specialized duties and responsibilities. *Biomedical equipment technicians* work with instruments used during medical procedures. They receive special training in the biomedical area in which their instruments are used.

Calibration technicians, also known as *standards laboratory technicians,* work in the electronics industry and in aerospace and aircraft manufacturing. As part of their inspection of systems and instruments, they measure parts for conformity to specifications, and they help develop calibration standards, devise formulas to solve problems in measurement and calibration, and write procedures and practical guides for other calibration technicians.

Electromechanical technicians work with automated mechanical equipment controlled by electronic sensing devices. They assist mechanical engineers in the design and development of such equipment, analyze test results, and write reports. The technician follows blueprints, operates metalworking machines, builds instrument housings, installs electrical equipment, and calibrates instruments and machinery. Technicians who specialize in the assembly of prototype instruments are known as *development technicians. Fabrication technicians* specialize in the assembly of production instruments.

Nuclear instrumentation technicians work with instruments at a nuclear power plant. These instruments control the various systems within the nuclear reactor, detect radiation, and sound alarms in case of equipment failure. *Instrument sales technicians* work for equipment manufacturing companies. They analyze customer needs, outline specifications for equipment cost and function, and sometimes do emergency troubleshooting.

REQUIREMENTS

High School
Math and science courses, such as algebra, geometry, physics, and chemistry, are essential prerequisites to becoming an instrumentation technician. In addition, machine and electrical shop courses will help you become familiar with electrical, mechanical, and electronic technology. Classes in mechanical drawing and computer-aided drafting are also beneficial. Instrumentation technicians also need good writing and communication skills, so be sure to take English, composition, and speech classes.

Postsecondary Training
The basic requirement for an entry-level job is completion of a two-year technical program or equivalent experience in a related field. Such equivalent experience may come from work in an electronics or manufacturing firm or any job that provides experience working with mechanical or electrical equipment.

Technical programs beyond high school can be found in community colleges as well as technical schools. Programs are offered in many different disciplines in addition to instrumentation technology. Programs may be in electronics or in electrical, mechanical, biomedical, or nuclear technology.

Most programs allow technicians to develop hands-on and laboratory skills as well as learn theory. Classes are likely to include instruction on electronic circuitry, computer science, mathematics, and physics. Courses in basic electronics, electrical theory, and graphics are also important. Technical writing is helpful as most technicians will prepare technical reports. Industrial economics, applied psychology, and plant management courses are helpful to those who plan to move into customer service or design.

Certification or Licensing
Instrumentation technicians who graduate from a recognized technical program may become certified by the National Institute for Certification in Engineering Technologies, although this is usually not a required part of a job. Certification is available at various levels, each combining a written exam in one of more than 25 specialty fields with a specified amount of job-related experience. Instrumentation

technicians who specialize in biomedical equipment repair can receive voluntary certification from the Board of Examiners for Biomedical Equipment Technicians. The International Society of Automation also offers certification for technicians who are involved in automation, control, maintenance, and manufacturing.

Other Requirements

To be an instrumentation technician, you need mathematical and scientific aptitude and the patience to methodically pursue complex questions. A tolerance for following prescribed procedures is essential, especially when undertaking assignments requiring a very precise, unchanging system of problem solving. Successful instrumentation technicians are able to provide solutions quickly and accurately even in stressful situations.

EXPLORING

As a way to test your abilities and learn more about calibration work try building small electronic equipment. Kits for building radios and other small appliances are available in some electronics shops. This will give you a basic understanding of electronic components and applications.

Some communities and schools also have clubs for people interested in electronics. They may offer classes that teach basic skills in construction, repair, and adjustment of electrical and electronic products. Model building, particularly in hard plastic and steel, will give you a good understanding of how to adapt and fit parts together. It may also help develop your hand skills if you want to work with precision instruments.

Visits to industrial laboratories, instrument shops, research laboratories, power installations, and manufacturing companies that rely on automated processes can expose you to the activities of instrumentation technicians. During such visits, you might be able to speak with technicians about their work or with managers about possible openings in their company. Also, you might look into getting a summer or part-time job as a helper on an industrial maintenance crew.

EMPLOYERS

Employers of instrumentation technicians include oil refineries, chemical and industrial laboratories, electronics firms, aircraft and aeronautical manufacturers, and biomedical firms. Companies involved in space exploration, oceanographic research, and national defense systems also employ instrumentation technicians. In addition, they work in various capacities in such industries as automotives, food, metals, ceramics, pulp and paper, power, textiles, pharmaceuticals, mining, metals, and pollution control.

STARTING OUT

Many companies recruit students prior to their graduation. Chemical and medical research companies especially need maintenance and operations technicians and usually recruit at schools where training in these areas is strong. Similarly, many industries in search of design technicians recruit at technical institutes and community colleges where the program is likely to meet their needs.

Students may also get assistance in their job searches through their schools' career services office, or they may learn about openings through ads in the newspapers. Prospective employees can also apply directly to a company in which they are interested.

ADVANCEMENT

Entry-level technicians develop their skills by learning tasks on their employers' equipment. Those with good academic records may, upon completion of an employer's basic program, move to an advanced level in sales or another area where a general understanding of the field is more important than specific laboratory skills. Technicians who have developed proficiency in instrumentation may choose to move to a supervisory or specialized position that requires knowledge of a particular aspect of instrumentation.

EARNINGS

Earnings for instrumentation technicians vary by industry, geographic region, educational background, experience, and level of responsibility. According to the U.S. Department of Labor, median annual earnings of electromechanical technicians were $48,110 in 2008. Salaries ranged from less than $25,580 to more than $71,380. Electrical and electronic engineering technicians had median annual earnings of $53,990 in 2008, and mechanical engineering technicians earned $50,040. Medical equipment repairers earned average salaries of $44,030.

Employee benefits vary, but can include paid vacations and holidays, sick leave, insurance benefits, 401(k) plans, profit sharing, pension plans, and tuition assistance programs.

WORK ENVIRONMENT

Working conditions vary widely for instrumentation technicians. An oil refinery plant job is as different from space mission instrumentation work as a nuclear reactor instrumentation job is different from work in the operating room of a hospital. All these jobs use similar principles, however, and instrumentation technicians can master new areas by applying what they have learned previously. For technicians who would like to travel, the petroleum industry, in particular, provides employment opportunities in foreign countries.

Instrumentation technicians' tasks may range from the routine to the highly complex and challenging. A calm, professional approach to work is essential. Calibration and adjustment require the dexterity and control of a watchmaker. Consequently, a person who is easily excited or impatient is not well suited to this kind of employment.

OUTLOOK

Employment opportunities for most instrumentation technicians will grow about as fast as the average for all occupations through 2018. Opportunities will be best for graduates of postsecondary technical training programs. As technology becomes more sophisticated, employers will continue to look for technicians who are skilled in new technology and require a minimum of additional job training.

Most developments in automated manufacturing techniques, including robotics and computer-controlled machinery, rely heavily on instrumentation devices. The emerging fields of air and water pollution control are other areas of growth. Scientists and technicians measure the amount of toxic substances in the air or test water with the use of instrumentation.

Oceanography, including the search for undersea deposits of oil and minerals, is another expanding field for instrumentation technology, as is medical diagnosis, including long-distance diagnosis by physicians through the use of sensors, computers, and Internet-based telecommunication.

One important field of growth is the teaching profession. As demand rises for skilled technicians, qualified instructors with combined knowledge of theory and application will be needed. Opportunities already exist, not only in educational institutions but also in those industries that have internal training programs.

FOR MORE INFORMATION

For a list of accredited technology programs, contact
Accreditation Board for Engineering and Technology
111 Market Place, Suite 1050
Baltimore, MD 21202-4012
Tel: 410-347-7700
http://www.abet.org

For information on educational programs and medical instrument certification, contact
Association for the Advancement of Medical Instrumentation
1110 North Glebe Road, Suite 220
Arlington, VA 22201-4795
Tel: 703-525-4890
Email: certifications@aami.org
http://www.aami.org

For information on careers and accredited programs, contact
Institute of Electrical and Electronics Engineers
1828 L Street, NW, Suite 1202
Washington, DC 20036-5104
Tel: 202-785-0017
Email: ieeeusa@ieee.org
http://www.ieee.org

For information on certification, careers, and student membership, contact
International Society of Automation
67 Alexander Drive
Research Triangle Park, NC 27709
Tel: 919-549-8411
Email: info@isa.org
http://www.isa.org

For information on careers and student clubs, contact
Junior Engineering Technical Society
1420 King Street, Suite 405
Alexandria, VA 22314-2750
Tel: 703-548-5387
Email: info@jets.org
http://www.jets.org

For information on certification, contact
National Institute for Certification in Engineering Technologies
1420 King Street
Alexandria, VA 22314-2750
Tel: 888-IS-NICET
http://www.nicet.org

Laser Technicians

OVERVIEW

Laser technicians produce, install, operate, service, and test laser systems and fiber optics equipment in industrial, medical, or research settings. They work under the direction of engineers or physicists who conduct laboratory activities in laser research and development or design. Depending upon the type of laser system—gas or solid state—a technician generally works either with information systems or with robotics, manufacturing, or medical equipment.

HISTORY

The laser was invented in 1958 by the American physicist Gordon Gould. The first working model was a ruby laser, designed and built by Dr. Ted Maiman in 1960. This first working laser created great interest in scientific research laboratories and started intensive experimentation and development in the field of electro-optics.

The word *laser* is actually an acronym for light amplification by stimulated emission of radiation. The laser converts electrical power into a special beam of optical or light power. Laser light is different from white light, or light that is produced by ordinary sources. It travels in a parallel beam, diffusing much less than white light. It is also composed of a single color wavelength as opposed to the jumble of colored light waves that make up white light. Because of these unique properties, laser light can be used in a number of different ways.

After its discovery, engineers and scientists considered using the light beam's power in the same ways as electrical power. From 1960 to 1967, various new lasers and electro-optic devices and techniques were developed. Some had considerable optical power, while others had only a small amount of power.

It soon became clear that lasers could be used to solve problems that previously had no practical solution. For example, concentrated beams of laser light are so powerful that they could drill tiny holes in diamonds, taking minutes where old methods took days.

Lasers began to be used in practical applications, such as surgery, surveying and measuring, industrial product inspection and testing, computers, microprocessors, and manufacturing. As lasers moved from research laboratories to industry, a need arose for workers who were trained in the practical application and technical aspects of the field. In the early 1970s two-year technical institutes and community colleges began offering specialized training programs in laser technology. The position of laser technician has become a valuable and necessary one in many industries, medical settings, and research programs.

THE JOB

There are basically two types of laser systems with which laser technicians work: *semiconductor laser systems,* which are the most compact and reliable, and *gas-type lasers,* which are larger and more expensive.

Laser technicians working with semiconductor systems are involved mainly with computer and telephone systems. In addition to helping to test, install, and maintain these systems, technicians work with engineers in their design and improvement.

Technicians who work with gas-type systems usually assist scientists, engineers, or doctors. These systems are used primarily in the fields of robotics, manufacturing, and medical procedures.

Laser technicians perform a wide variety of tasks. Much depends upon their positions and places of employment. For example, some repair lasers and instruct companies on their use, while others work as technicians for very specific applications, such as optical surgery or welding parts.

In general, most technicians are employed in one of five areas: materials processing, communications, military, medical, and research. Technicians are involved in building laser devices in any one of these fields. To build a solid-state laser, they construct, cut, and polish a crystal rod to be used in the laser. They put a flash tube around the crystal and place the unit in a container with a mirror at each end. Using precision instruments, they position the mirrors so that all emitted or reflected light passes through the crystal. Finally, they put the laser body in a chassis, install tubing and wiring to the controls, and place a jacket around the assembly.

There are other duties that all technicians perform, no matter what application they work in. These include taking measurements, cleaning, aligning, inspecting, and operating lasers, and collecting data. Since the laser field is so technologically advanced, computers are used in many tasks and applications. Technicians may be responsible for programming the computers that control the lasers, for inputting data, or for generating reports.

In materials processing, lasers are used for machining, production, measurement, construction, excavation, and photo-optics. Technicians often read and interpret diagrams, schematics, and shop drawings in order to assemble components themselves or oversee the assembly process. They may operate lasers for welding, precision drilling, cutting, and grinding of metal parts, or for trimming and slicing electronic components and circuit elements. They may use lasers to verify precise parts sizes. Finally, technicians may be involved in part marking—using a laser to mark an identifying number or letter on each component. In construction, they may use a laser as a surveying guideline or an aligning tool.

Laser technicians in communications use lasers to generate light impulses transmitted through optical fibers. They help to develop, manufacture, and test optical equipment, and they may design, set up, monitor, and maintain fiber fabrication facilities. This field also uses lasers for data storage and retrieval.

In military and space projects, lasers are frequently used for target finding, tracking, ranging, identification, and communications. Technicians repair and adapt low-power lasers, which are widely used for these applications.

In medical applications, technicians serve as technical equipment experts and assist physicians and surgeons who use the laser system. They advise on which type of laser and method of delivery to use. They must be on hand during laser procedures to offer recommendations, fine-tune attachments and machines, and troubleshoot if a technical problem occurs.

In research and development, lasers are being studied as a source of high-intensity heat in controlled nuclear fusion. These studies are part of the continuing research to produce inexpensive electrical power. Technicians on any research and development team use lasers and electronic devices to perform tests, take measurements, gather data, and make calculations. They may prepare reports for engineers, doctors, scientists, production managers, or lab workers.

REQUIREMENTS
High School
You can prepare for this career by taking four years of English and at least two years of mathematics, one of which should be algebra. At least one year of physical science, preferably physics, should be included, as well as a class in basic computer programming. Machine shop, basic electronics, and blueprint reading classes are also useful.

Postsecondary Training
Most laser technicians enter the field after attending a two-year program in laser technology at a vocational, technical, or community college. The average associate's degree program in laser technology includes intensive technical and scientific study, with more hours spent in a laboratory or work situation than in the actual classroom. This hands-on experience is supplemented in the first year by courses in mathematics, physics, drafting, diagramming, basic electronics, electronic instrumentation and calibration, introduction to solid-state devices, electromechanical controls, and computer programming.

The second year of study might include courses in geometrical optics, digital circuits, microwaves, laser and electro-optic components, devices and measurements, vacuum techniques, technical report writing, microcomputers, and computer hardware. Special laser projects are often a part of the second year and can help you decide on a specific field. Even after completing your education, you will probably need further training depending on your employer's requirements.

Certification and Licensing
Voluntary certification for laser technicians who repair medical equipment is available from the National Council on Laser Excellence.

Other Requirements
You must have an interest in instruments, laboratory apparatus, and how devices and systems work. Written and spoken communications are very important since you often have to work closely with people of varied technological backgrounds.

Physical strength is not usually required, but good manual dexterity and hand–eye and body coordination are quite important. Because lasers can be extremely dangerous, you must be careful, attentive, and willing to follow safety precautions closely. The ability to work efficiently, patiently, and consistently is extremely important, as is the ability to solve problems and do careful, detailed work.

Typical Classes for Laser Technology Students

- Advanced Circuits and Systems
- Advanced Laser Topics
- Applied Optics
- Computer-Aided Drafting
- Electric Circuits and Systems
- Fiber Optics
- Introduction to Lasers
- Introduction to Photonics
- Laser and Lab Safety
- Laser Electronics
- Optoelectronics
- Physics Mechanics
- Technical Writing

EXPLORING

Talk to your school counselor about careers in laser technology. If you live near a community or technical college that offers programs in laser technology, visit the institution and talk with counselors and teachers. In addition, review some of the periodicals that are devoted to the field of lasers. Periodicals such as the *Journal of Laser Applications* (http:// scitation.aip.org/jla/) and *Laser Focus World* (www. laserfocusworld.com) may offer valuable insight into the field.

Lasers are used in so many places that it should be fairly easy to find a local laser technician, operator, or engineer who can share knowledge about his or her job. It might be possible to find summer or part-time work in construction, manufacturing, or mining where lasers are used in measuring, cutting and welding, and surveying. This type of work can give you a look at jobs in laser technology.

EMPLOYERS

Laser technicians work in manufacturing, communications, medicine, scientific research, the military, and construction.

STARTING OUT

Colleges that offer associate's degrees in laser technology usually work closely with industry, providing their graduating students with placement services and lists of potential employers. Most laser technicians graduating from a two-year program, in fact, are interviewed and recruited while still in school by representatives of companies that need laser technicians. If hired, they begin working soon after graduation.

Another way to enter the career is to join a branch of the U.S. Armed Forces under a technical training program for laser technicians. Military laser training is not always compatible with civilian training, however, and further study of theory and applications may be needed to enter the field as a civilian.

Additionally, the Laser Institute of America offers job listings at its Web site (http://careers.laserinstitute.org/search).

ADVANCEMENT

Opportunities for advancement in laser technology are excellent for technicians who keep up with advances in the field. In such a relatively new technology, developments occur very rapidly. Workers who learn about and adapt to these changes become more valuable to their employers and advance to greater responsibilities.

Many employers designate various grades or levels for laser technicians, according to experience, education, and job performance. By being promoted through these levels, technicians can advance to supervisory or managerial positions. Supervisors manage a department, supervise other technicians, and train new or current employees.

Mature, experienced, and highly successful laser technicians may become consultants or specialists for individual firms. A consulting position entails working closely with clients, conducting studies and surveys, and proposing improvements, changes, and solutions to problems.

Some technicians move into sales or technical writing positions. Others become instructors in vocational programs, teaching intermediate or advanced laser and fiber optics technology courses.

EARNINGS

According to a survey done by the Laser Institute of America, the average starting salary for laser technicians is approximately $25,000 per year. Salaries for technicians with at least five years of experience average approximately $30,000 per year, depending on background, experience, and the industry where they are employed. Laser technicians with considerable experience can earn salaries that range from $46,000 to more than $67,000 annually.

In addition to salary, technicians usually receive benefits such as insurance, paid holidays and vacations, and retirement plans. Many employers have liberal policies of paying for professional improvement through continued study in school or at work.

WORK ENVIRONMENT

Working conditions for laser technicians vary according to the industry. Some technicians spend their day in a laboratory, while others work in a hospital operating room, office, or manufacturing plant. In most cases, however, work areas are kept clean and temperature controlled in order to protect the laser equipment.

Laser technicians may work at relatively stationary jobs, assembling or operating lasers in the same environment every day, or they may be required to move around frequently, in and out of laboratory areas, production sites, or offices. Some technicians are office or laboratory based; others, especially those in sales and service positions, may travel the country.

Laser technicians typically work regular hours. Five eight-hour days per week is the standard, although certain projects may occasionally require overtime.

There are possible hazards in most areas where lasers are used. Because the power supplies for many lasers involve high voltages, technicians frequently work around potentially deadly amounts of electricity. The laser beam itself is also a possible source of serious injury, either through direct exposure to the beam or by reflected light from the laser. Safety precautions, such as wearing protective glasses, are strictly enforced.

Laser technicians handle extremely valuable instruments. The parts used to make lasers are almost always costly. Mistakes that damage lasers or errors in applying lasers can be very costly, running into the thousands of dollars.

Technicians often work as part of a production team or supervisory group, sometimes with scientists and engineers, sometimes as a member of a production team or supervisory group. Some technicians work alone but usually report directly to an engineer, scientist, or manager.

Among the greatest sources of satisfaction for laser technicians is the feeling of success whenever they meet a challenge and see their laser systems perform correctly. This is especially true in sales and service where new users are taught to use this complicated technology and where the technician can actually see customers discovering the effectiveness of lasers. The same satisfaction is felt in research when a new development is proved to be a success.

OUTLOOK

Employment opportunities for laser technicians are expected to be good over the next several years. Rapid changes in technology and continued growth in the industry will almost certainly lead to an increase in the number of technicians employed. Currently the demand far outweighs the supply of qualified laser technicians.

One of the fastest growing areas for laser technicians is fiber optic systems that are used in communications. Optical fiber is replacing wire cables in communication lines and in many electronic products. This trend is expected to continue, so the demand for technicians in the fiber optics field should be especially strong. Growth is also expected to be strong in production, defense, medicine, and construction. Technicians interested in research and development, however, should keep in mind that job growth often slows in the face of economic downturns.

FOR MORE INFORMATION

For information on laser technology and student chapters, contact
IEEE Laser and Electro-Optics Society
445 Hoes Lane
Piscataway, NJ 08855-1331
http://www.i-leos.org

For information on becoming a laser technician, contact
Laser Institute of America
13501 Ingenuity Drive, Suite 128
Orlando, FL 32826
Tel: 800-345-2737
Email: lia@laserinstitute.org
http://www.laserinstitute.org

For information on certification, contact
National Council on Laser Excellence
PO Box 997
Grove City, OH 43123-0997
Tel: 800-435-3131
http://www.lasercertification.org

INTERVIEW

Bill Gray and Frank Reed are laser instructors in the Laser/Electro-Optics Technology Program at Indian Hills Community College

(IHCC) in Ottumwa, Iowa. Students who complete the 21-month program are awarded an associate in applied science degree. Gray and Reed spoke with the editors of Careers in Focus: Technicians *about careers in laser technology and their school's program.*

Q. What is laser/electro-optics technology?

A. A study in all things light-based—from Abbe condenser to Z-scan with emphasis on lasers and optics.

Q. What common misconceptions do people have about this field of study?

A. The only misconception we can think of is the myth or mindset that laser technology is "too difficult." EVERY student at Indian Hills, at least for the past 10 years, who comes to class and does work in the lab, has passed and has a super job.

Also, our program is not just about laser technology. The laser is only one part of what the students learn. We teach photonics, which is anything that has to do with a photon: light, imaging, detection, display, industrial applications, medical applications, LEDs [light emitting diodes], military, space, and especially optics.

Q. Can you tell us about some of the typical classes that are required in your program?

A.

- **LEO101 Photonics Concepts 4**. This course introduces the student to the way light is generated and manipulated. Students perform basic labs to enhance their understanding of optics and laser beams. Laser industry experts discuss real world applications and the future of the photonics industry.
- **LEO242 Introduction to Photonics 4**. This course covers the history, safety, and theory of laser light and laser systems. Different laser system configurations and operations are examined.
- **LEO250 Automated Laser Processing 3**. This course covers the basics of laser material processing. Students perform laser welding, drilling, cutting, and marking of various materials. The properties of materials and the interaction of the laser light with the materials is the focus. Statistical process control, blueprint reading, and CNC (Computer Numerical Control) of laser systems are strongly emphasized.
- **LEO253 Physical Optics 2**. This course is designed to teach students wave theory of light. Reflection and refraction

of waves are demonstrated analytically and graphically. Interference, wave propagation, diffraction, holography, polarization, and other effects are studied.

- **LEO255 Geometric Optics 4**. This course is designed to provide students with an understanding of geometric ray and particle theory of light. The laws of reflection and refraction from mathematical, geometrical, and experimental aspects are studied.
- **LEO257 Laser Components 2**. This course covers the equipment and hardware used with lasers and laser systems. Different types of laser systems and equipment are discussed.
- **LEO259 Optical Devices 3**. This course teaches students the operational theory behind equipment used for laser beam measurement and manipulation. Students work with detectors, beam expanders/collimators, holography, and acoustic and electro-optic devices.
- **LEO262 Laser System Fundamentals 3**. This course is an in-depth study of solid-state, ion, gas, molecular, and semiconductor lasers and laser systems. Diode pumped solid-state lasers, Q-switching, and other laser output measurements are covered.

Q. What are the most important qualities for students in your program?

A. To be successful, students must have good interpersonal skills, the ability to learn, problem-solving abilities, good attendance/punctuality, honesty/integrity, and good communication skills. The employers who hire our students know they will have a great technical foundation after 21 months at IHCC.

Q. The study of laser/electro-optics technology prepares students for what types of jobs?

A. Our students are hired directly out of school as laser technicians, optical technicians, field service engineers, sales engineers, quality control technicians, manufacturing technicians, maintenance technicians, and training specialists.

Q. What advice would you offer students as they graduate from your program and look for jobs?

A. Most students (those that want one) have jobs before they graduate. The best advice we have is, "You get out what you put in." When students first enter our program, we let them know that they are in training, like Olympic athletes. They are in a national competition for jobs. Have they ever trained for a national competition? It takes a considerable amount of effort early in the program. The harder they train (study) now, the better they'll do in the job hunt.

Also, students should know their support group and constraints. Family and friends have a huge influence on each student's job decision, as they should. Students need to ask themselves and their support group the following questions: Where in the nation or world do they want to work? What type of job are they looking for? How much pay and what benefits will they need or want?

Q. What changes in the job market should students expect?

A. There are always unexpected changes in the job market—usually good. Photonics is such a broad technology, if one industry is down, another is usually up. So our students have a wide range of companies and industries to pursue; there is always a job out there. We, really the students, contact so many new companies every year—they find out about us, we find out about them—and a new relationship begins. Here at IHCC we have a "diversified portfolio" of employers so when there is a downturn in one area another area is up and our students maintain high employability. In the past five years IHCC laser/optics graduates are averaging 14 job opportunities per student.

Our employers include medical companies, government contractors, research facilities, and laser base job shops.

Q. What is the future of your program?

A. The future of our program is stability with growth. The IHCC Laser/Optics Program has held steady for more than five years when other programs around the nation seem to be struggling or have closed their doors. We continue to have great job placement, and we do not see that slowing.

Microelectronics Technicians

OVERVIEW

Microelectronics technicians work in research laboratories assisting the engineering staff to develop and construct prototype and custom-designed microchips. Microchips, often called simply chips, are tiny but extremely complex electronic devices that control the operations of many kinds of communications equipment, consumer products, industrial controls, aerospace guidance systems, and medical electronics. The process of manufacturing chips is often called fabrication. Microelectronics technicians are often classified under the career category electrical and electronics engineering technicians. About 164,000 people work as electrical and electronics engineering technicians.

HISTORY

The science of electronics is only about 100 years old. Yet electronics has had an enormous impact on the way people live. Without electronics, things like television, mobile phones, computers, X-ray machines, and radar would not be possible. Today, nearly every area of industry, manufacturing, entertainment, health care, and communications uses electronics to improve the quality of people's lives. This book you are reading, for example, was created by people using electronic equipment to write, design, edit, and produce the book itself.

The earliest electronic systems depended on electron vacuum tubes to conduct current. But these devices were too bulky and too slow for many of their desired tasks. In the early 1950s the intro-

QUICK FACTS

School Subjects
English
Mathematics
Physics

Personal Skills
Mechanical/manipulative
Technical/scientific

Work Environment
Primarily indoors
Primarily one location

Minimum Education Level
Associate's degree

Salary Range
$32,490 to $53,240 to $85,000

Certification or Licensing
Voluntary

Outlook
Little or no change

DOT
590

GOE
08.02.02

NOC
9483

O*NET-SOC
17-3023.00

duction of microelectronics—that is, the design and production of integrated circuits and products using integrated circuits—allowed engineers and scientists to design faster and faster and smaller and smaller electronic devices. Initially developed for military equipment and space technology, integrated circuits have made possible such everyday products as personal computers, microwave ovens, and digital video disc players and are found in nearly every electronic product that people use today.

Integrated circuits are miniaturized electronic systems. Integrated circuits include many interconnected electronic components such as transistors, capacitors, and resistors, produced on or in a single thin slice of a semiconductor material. Semiconductors are so named because they are substances with electrical properties somewhere between those of conductors and insulators. The semiconductor used most frequently in microchips is silicon, so microchips are also sometimes called silicon chips. Often smaller than a fingernail, chips may contain multiple layers of complex circuitry stacked on top of each other. The word integrated refers to the way the circuitry is blended into the chip during the fabrication process.

The reliance on electronic technology has created a need for skilled personnel to design, construct, test, and repair electronic components and products. The growing uses of microelectronics has created a corresponding demand for technicians specially trained to assist in the design and development of new applications of electronic technology.

THE JOB

Microelectronics technicians typically assist in the development of prototypes, or new kinds, of electronic components and products. They work closely with electronics engineers, who design the components, build and test them, and prepare the component or product for large-scale manufacture. Such components usually require the integrated operation of several or many different types of chips.

Microelectronics technicians generally work from a schematic received from the design engineer. The schematic contains a list of the parts that will be needed to construct the component and the layout that the technician will follow. The technician gathers the parts and prepares the materials to be used. Following the schematic, the technician constructs the component and then uses a variety of sophisticated, highly sensitive equipment to test the component's performance. One such test measures the component's burn-in time. During this test the component is kept in continuous operation for a long period of time, and the component and its various features are subjected to a variety of tests to be certain the component will stand up to extended use.

If the component fails to function according to its required specifications, the microelectronics technician must be able to troubleshoot the design, locating where the component has failed, and replace one part for a new or different part. Test results are reported to the engineering staff, and the technician may be required to help evaluate the results and prepare reports based on these evaluations. In many situations, the microelectronics technician will work closely with the engineer to solve any problems arising in the component's operation and design.

After the testing period, the microelectronics technician is often responsible for assisting in the technical writing of the component's specifications. These specifications are used for integrating the component into new or redesigned products or for developing the process for the component's large-scale manufacture. The microelectronics technician helps to develop the production system for the component and will also write reports on the component's functions, uses, and performance.

"You really need to have good communication skills," says Kyle Turner, a microelectronics technician at White Oak Semiconductor in Virginia. "Not only do you have to let others know what you mean and explain yourself, you often have to train new employees in the specifics of our product."

Microelectronics technicians perform many of the same functions of electronics technicians, but generally work only in the development laboratory. More experienced technicians may assume greater responsibilities. They work closely with the engineering staff to develop layout and assembly procedures and to use their own knowledge of microelectronics to suggest changes in circuitry or installation. Often they are depended upon to simplify the assembly or maintenance requirements. After making any changes, they test the performance of the component, analyze the results, and suggest and perform further modifications to the component's design. Technicians may fabricate new parts using various machine tools, supervise the installation of the new component, or become involved in training and supervising other technical personnel.

Some microelectronics technicians specialize in the fabrication and testing of semiconductors and integrated circuits. These technicians are usually called *semiconductor development technicians*. Following the direction of engineering staff, they are involved in the development of prototype chips and perform the various steps required for making and testing new integrated circuits.

REQUIREMENTS

The advanced technology involved in microelectronics means that post–high school education or training is a requirement for entering the field. You should consider enrolling in a two-year training program at a community college or vocational training facility and expect to earn a certificate or an associate's degree. Like most microelectronics technicians, Kyle Turner completed a two-year degree in electronics as well as an extensive on-the-job training program.

High School

High school students interested in microelectronics can begin their preparation by taking courses such as algebra and geometry. If you have taken science courses, especially chemistry and physics, you will have a better chance to enter an apprenticeship program and you will be more prepared for postsecondary educational programs.

"Math skills are really important," says Turner. "You have to be able to take accurate measurements and make good calculations."

Knowledge of proper grammar and spelling is necessary for writing reports, and you should also develop your reading comprehension. Taking industrial classes, such as metalworking, wood shop, auto shop, and machine shop, and similar courses in plastics, electronics, and construction techniques will be helpful. Another area of study is computer science; you would do well to seek experience in computer technology.

Postsecondary Training

Few employers will hire people for microelectronics technician positions who do not have advanced training. Although some low-skilled workers may advance into technician jobs, employers generally prefer to hire people with higher education. Technician and associate's degree programs are available at many community colleges and at public and private vocational training centers and schools. Many technical schools are located where the microelectronics industry is particularly active. These schools often have programs tailored specifically for the needs of companies in their area. Community colleges offer a greater degree of flexibility in that they are able to keep up with the rapid advances and changes in technology and can redesign their courses and programs to meet the new requirements. You can expect to study in such areas as mathematics, including algebra, geometry, and calculus; physics; and electronics engineering technology. Many schools will require you to take courses in English composition, as well as fulfill other course requirements in the humanities and social sciences.

Other methods of entry are three- and four-year apprenticeship programs. These programs generally involve on-the-job training by the employer. You can locate apprenticeship opportunities through your high school guidance office, in listings in local newspapers, or by contacting local manufacturers.

Military service is also an excellent method for beginning an electronics career. The military is one of the largest users of electronics technology and offers training and educational programs to enlisted personnel in many areas of electronics.

Finally, the rapid advancements in microelectronics may make it desirable or even necessary for you to continue to take courses, receive training, and study various trade journals throughout your career.

Certification or Licensing

Certification is not mandatory in most areas of electronics (although technicians working with radio-transmitting devices are required to be licensed by the Federal Communications Commission), but voluntary certification may prove useful in locating work and in increasing your pay and responsibilities. The International Society of Certified Electronics Technicians (ISCET) offers certification testing to technicians with experience or schooling, as well as associate-level testing of basic electronics for beginning technicians. ISCET also offers a variety of study and training materials to help you prepare for the certification tests. Electronics Technicians Association International also provides certification.

Other Requirements

Microelectronics technicians are involved in creating prototypes—that is, new and untested technology. This aspect of the field brings special responsibilities for carrying out assembly and testing procedures: These must be performed with a high degree of precision. When assembling a new component, for example, you must be able to follow the design engineer's specifications and instructions exactly. Similar diligence and attention to detail are necessary when following the different procedures for testing the new components. An understanding of the underlying technology is important.

EXPLORING

You can begin exploring this field by getting involved in science clubs and working on electronics projects at home. Any part-time experience repairing electronic equipment will give you exposure to the basics of electronics.

Books to Read

Boysen, Earl, and Nancy C. Muir. *Electronics Projects For Dummies*. Hoboken, N.J.: For Dummies, 2006.

Gibilisco, Stan. *Teach Yourself Electricity and Electronics*. 4th ed. New York: McGraw-Hill/TAB Electronics, 2006.

McComb, Gordon. *Electronics For Dummies*. 2d ed. Hoboken, N.J.: For Dummies, 2009.

Razavi, Behzad. *Fundamentals of Microelectronics*. Hoboken, N.J.: Wiley, 2008.

Silver, H. Ward. *Circuitbuilding Do-It-Yourself For Dummies*. Hoboken, N.J.: For Dummies, 2008.

Whitaker, Jerry C. *Microelectronics*. 2d ed. Boca Raton, Fla.: CRC Press, 2005.

You can find many resources for electronics experiments and projects in your school or local library or on the Internet. Summer employment in any type of electronics will be useful. Talking with someone who works in the field may help you narrow your focus to one particular area of electronics.

EMPLOYERS

Many of the 164,000 electrical and electronics engineering technicians employed in the United States work in the computers, electronics, and communications fields. Because these fields are geographically concentrated in Arizona, Oregon, and Massachusetts, many electronics technician jobs are located in these areas. There are positions available elsewhere, but many technicians relocate to work in these concentrated areas. Some electronics technicians are self-employed, some work for large corporations, and others work in government-related jobs.

STARTING OUT

Most schools provide job placement services to students completing their degree program. Many offer on-the-job training as a part of the program. An internship or other real-life experience is desirable but not necessary. Many companies have extensive on-site training programs.

Newspapers and trade journals are full of openings for people working in electronics, and some companies recruit new hires directly on campus. Government employment offices are also good sources when looking for job leads.

ADVANCEMENT

Microelectronics technicians who choose to continue their education can expect to increase their responsibilities and be eligible to advance to supervisory and managerial positions.

Microelectronics technicians may also desire to enter other, more demanding areas of microelectronics, such as semiconductor development and engineering. Additional education may be necessary; engineers will be required to hold at least a four-year degree in electronics engineering.

Earning certification may be part of the requirement for advancement in certain companies.

EARNINGS

According to the U.S. Department of Labor, median annual earnings of electrical and electronics engineering technicians were $53,240 in 2007. Salaries ranged from less than $32,490 to more than $78,560. Mean annual earnings of technicians who worked in the semiconductor and other electronic component manufacturing industry were $50,730 in 2008. Those in managerial or supervisory positions earn higher salaries, ranging between $55,000 and $85,000 per year. Wage rates vary greatly, according to skill level, type of employer, and location. Most employers offer some fringe benefits, including paid holidays and vacations, sick leave, and life and health insurance.

WORK ENVIRONMENT

Microelectronics technicians generally work a 40-hour week, although they may be assigned to different shifts or be required to work weekends and holidays. Overtime and holiday pay can usually be expected in such circumstances. The work setting is extremely clean, well lighted, and dust free.

Microelectronics technicians have many duties, and this requires them to be flexible yet focused as they perform their duties. They have to be exact and precise in their work no matter what they're doing, whether building an electronic component, running the tests, or recording the data. The fact that each day is often very different from the one before it is an aspect of the job that many technicians find appealing.

"One of the best things about the job is that it's always changing. We're always trying to make a better product, reduce cycle time, make it smaller or cheaper," says Kyle Turner. "You're always learning because it changes like crazy."

OUTLOOK

Employment in the electronics industry is expected to experience little or no change through 2018, according to the U.S. Department of Labor. The increasing reliability and durability of electronic technology will have a negative effect on the need for technicians. Similarly, increasing imports of microelectronics products, components, and technology may represent a decrease in production in the United States, which will in turn decrease the numbers of microelectronics technicians needed here. Additionally, the use of advanced technologies, such as computer-aided design and drafting and computer simulation, will improve worker productivity and limit employment growth. The government will continue to account for a large part of the demand for microelectronics components, technology, and personnel.

FOR MORE INFORMATION

For information on certification, contact
Electronics Technicians Association International
Five Depot Street
Greencastle, IN 46135-8024
Tel: 800-288-3824
Email: eta@eta-i.org
http://www.eta-i.org

For information on certification and student chapters, contact
International Society of Certified Electronics Technicians
3608 Pershing Avenue
Fort Worth, TX 76107-4527
Tel: 800-946-0201
Email: info@iscet.org
http://www.iscet.org

For information on semiconductors, a glossary of terms, and industry information, contact
Semiconductor Industry Association
181 Metro Drive, Suite 450
San Jose, CA 95110-1344
Tel: 408-436-6600
Email: mailbox@sia-online.org
http://www.sia-online.org

Optics Technicians

OVERVIEW

Optics technicians design, fabricate, assemble, or install optical instruments, such as telescopes, microscopes, aerial cameras, and eyeglasses. The four most common types of optics technicians are *optomechanical technicians, precision-lens technicians, precision-lens grinders* (sometimes called *optical technicians*), and *photo-optics technicians*.

In general, these four careers may be distinguished from one another in the following ways: Optomechanical technicians build and test complete optical and optomechanical devices. Precision-lens technicians handle the whole range of manufacturing activities to fabricate the lenses that go into optical and optomechanical devices. Precision-lens grinders grind, polish, cement, and inspect the lens. Photo-optics technicians install, maintain, or actually use the optical or optomechanical devices for scientific and engineering measurements and projects.

HISTORY

Humans have been using simple lenses for magnification for more than 1,000 years, and eyeglasses have been in use since the 14th century. More complex optical instruments, however, such as the microscope and telescope, were not developed until the 17th century. These first microscopes and telescopes were crude by modern standards, as the first lenses of moderately good quality for these instruments were not developed until the 19th century.

During the 19th century, many of the basic principles used for making the calculations necessary for lens design were expounded, first in an 1841 book by Karl Friedrich Gauss, and later in other studies, based on Gauss's work, published during the 1850s. These principles remained the basis for making the calculations needed for lens design until around 1960, when computer modeling became the predominant way to design lenses.

Up until the early part of the 20th century, engineering problems associated with the design of optical instruments were handled by mechanical engineers, physicists, and mathematicians. During World War I, however, because of the increasingly important applications of optical instruments, optical engineering emerged as a separate discipline, and today it is taught in a separate department in many universities.

Similarly, the optics technicians described in this article emerged as distinct from all other engineering and science technicians. They have their own instructional programs, their own professional societies, and their own licensing procedures.

THE JOB

The optical manufacturing industry offers many different types of jobs for the skilled and well-trained technician. There are jobs, especially for optomechanical technicians, that mostly involve scientific and theoretical matters. There are other jobs, such as those that precision-lens grinders often perform, that focus on craftworking skills. The work of precision-lens technicians, and for many other optics technicians as well, combines both of these kinds of activities. Finally, there are many jobs for optics technicians, but especially for photo-optics technicians, that require the mechanical skills and ingenuity of a repairer and troubleshooter.

In general, optics technicians are employed in one of the following areas: research and development, product manufacturing, maintenance and operations, and lens fabrication.

Technicians working in the research and development area seek to create new optical instruments or new applications for existing instruments. They are often called upon to invent new techniques to conduct experiments, obtain measurements, or carry out fabrication procedures requested by engineers or scientists.

Among the products that research-and-development technicians may be involved with are night-vision instruments for surveillance and security, ultraprecise distance-measuring devices, and instruments for analysis of medical and clinical specimens, monitoring patients, and routine inspection of materials including industrial wastes.

Technicians in the product-manufacturing area work mostly at the assembly, alignment, calibration, and testing of common optical instruments, such as microscopes, telescopes, binoculars, and cameras. They may also help produce less common devices, such as transits and levels for surveying or spectrographs and spectrophotometers used in medical research and diagnosis.

A relatively new field that allows both research-and-development technicians and product-development technicians opportunities to combine their interests in optics and photography is the development and production of integrated electronic circuits. These highly complex, tiny devices are used widely in calculators, computers, television equipment, and control devices for electronic systems, whether in the cockpit of a jet airliner or in the control room of an electric generating plant. The manufacture of these electronic circuits requires a wide variety of skills, from the production of large patterns and plans, called art work, to the alignment and operation of the microcameras that produce the extraordinarily small images used to make the final circuits on the tiny metallic chips that are the basis of the integrated circuits.

In the field of maintenance and operations, technicians are involved with the on-site use of optical instruments, such as technical and scientific cameras, large observatory telescopes and auxiliary instruments, light-measuring equipment, and spectrophotometers, some of which operate with invisible or ultraviolet radiation.

Operations and maintenance technicians (usually photo-optics technicians) may find themselves working at a rocket or missile test range or at a missile or satellite tracking station, where they may assemble, adjust, align, or operate telescopic cameras that produce some of the most important information about missiles in flight. These cameras are often as big as the telescopes used by astronomers, and they weigh up to 15 tons. Large, powerful motors enable the camera to rotate and, thus, to follow a rocket in flight until it comes down. The picture information gathered by these long-range tracking cameras is often the only clue to missile flight errors or failure, as there is often virtually nothing left of a missile after it lands.

Another kind of optics technician, called a *photonics technician,* works in a specialized area of optics called photonics. Photonics is a technology that uses photons, or particles of light, to process information. It includes lasers, fiber optics, optical instruments, and related electronics. Photonics technicians assist engineers in developing applications utilizing photonics. One such application is a wireless data communications network that links computer workstations through infrared technology. Photonics is being used in areas such as data communications, including using photons to send information through optical cables for telephone and computer communications, solar energy products, holograms, and compact discs.

In the lens-fabrication area there are many different kinds of jobs for optics technicians. *Lens molders* work with partially melted glass. Their principal task usually is to press the partially melted glass into rough lens blanks. *Lens blockers* assist senior lens makers in setting lens blanks into holders in preparation for curve generating, grinding, and polishing. *Lens generators*, using special grinding machines, give the glass blanks the correct curvature as they are held in the holders. *Lens grinders* work with cup-shaped tools and fine grinding powders. They bring the blanks in the holders to the required curve within close tolerances. *Lens polishers* use ultrafine powders and special tools made of pitch or beeswax to bring the surfaces of the fine-ground blank to bright, clear polish. *Lens centerers* or *lens edgers* make true, or perfect, the various optical elements with finished spherical surfaces. *Optical-coating technicians* carefully clean finished lenses and install them inside a vacuum chamber. Special mineral materials are then boiled in small, electrically heated vessels in the vacuum, and the vapor condenses on the lenses to form extremely thin layers that reduce glass surface reflections. *Quality inspectors* examine the finished lenses for tiny scratches, discolorations of the coating, and other faults or errors that may require rejection of the finished element before it is assembled into an instrument.

REQUIREMENTS

High School

If you are considering a career as an optics technician, you should take courses that provide a strong general background and prepare you for further study in technical fields, including mathematics, science, technical reading and writing, and shop. Courses in photography, particularly those involving darkroom work, are also valuable, since photography plays an important role in many fields where optics technicians work.

Postsecondary Training

There are only a few schools that offer specific training for optics technicians. A good alternate way to obtain advanced education is to attend a technical institute or community college where two- or three-year engineering or science programs are available and to pick out those courses best suited for a career as an optics technician.

During your first year of a two-year program, you should take courses in geometrical optics, trigonometry, lens polishing, technical writing, optical instruments, analytical geometry, and specifications writing. During your second year, you may take courses in physics, optical shop practices, manual preparation, mechanical drawing, and report preparation.

Some large corporations have training programs for beginning technicians. These programs are not always publicized and may take some searching to find. There are also some commercially run technical schools that provide training; however, they are often costly and should be investigated carefully, preferably by talking to former students, before undertaking such a program.

Certification or Licensing

Except for those optics technicians who not only make but dispense eyeglasses, there are no licensing requirements. However, in a few cases, optics technicians must be certified to manufacture and inspect instruments to be used in a government application or for medical or clinical purposes. In these instances, technicians should discuss any licensing or certification requirements with their employer or supervisor.

Other Requirements

To be an optics technician, you should have a strong interest in and a good aptitude for mathematics and physics. Patience, care, and good manual skills are important to design precision telescopic lenses, grind and polish the glass elements, and assemble and align the instrument.

EXPLORING

One of the best ways for students to gain experience in and exposure to the field of optics is through membership in a club or organization related to this field. These include hobby clubs, student societies, or groups with scientific interests. Some examples include the following: organizations for amateur astronomers, amateur radio builders and operators, and amateur telescope makers; and school photography clubs, especially those involving activities with film processing, print and enlargement making, and camera operations.

Through visits to industrial laboratories or manufacturing companies, you can witness technicians actually involved in their work and may be able to speak with several of these people regarding their work or with employers about possibilities for technicians in that particular industry or company.

EMPLOYERS

Optical grinding and polishing shops provide employment opportunities. Among the largest employers of optical technicians are the space program and weapons-development programs run by the military. Other employment opportunities are available with manufacturers of optical instruments, such as microscopes, telescopes, binoculars, cameras, and advanced medical equipment.

STARTING OUT

Many students enrolled in two-year training programs can find jobs through interviews with company recruiters conducted on campus during the second year of their program. Other students find employment through participation in work-study programs while enrolled in school. In many cases, the student's part-time employer will offer full-time work after graduation or provide leads on other possible jobs.

For students who do not find suitable employment in one of these ways, there are some employment agencies that specialize in placing personnel in the optics industry. There are also very active societies in the optical, photographic, physical science, and engineering fields that can be sources of worthwhile job leads. Contact technical societies for advice and help in job hunting. The primary purpose of a technical society is to aid the industry it represents, and there is no better way the society can do this than to attract interested people into the field and help them find a good job.

ADVANCEMENT

As technicians gain experience and additional skills, new and more demanding jobs are offered to them. The following paragraphs describe some of the jobs to which experienced technicians may advance.

Hand lens figurers shape some lenses and optical elements, using hand-operated grinding and polishing methods. These shapes are called "aspheric," as they cannot be made by the normal mass-production grinding and generating machines. Special highly sensitive test machines are used to aid these advanced polishing technicians.

Photographic technicians use the camera in many important research and engineering projects, as well as in the production of optical items such as reticles (cross hairs or wires in the focus of the eyepiece of an optical instrument), optical test targets, and integrated electronic circuits. These technicians will be involved in the operation of cameras and with photographic laboratory work, sometimes leading a team of technicians in these tasks.

Instrument assemblers and testers direct the assembly of various parts into the final instrument, performing certain critical assembly tasks themselves. When the instrument is complete, they, or other technicians under their direction, check the instrument's alignment, functioning, appearance, and readiness for the customer.

Optical model makers work with specially made or purchased components to assemble a prototype or first model of a new instrument under the direction of the engineer in charge. These technicians must be able to keep the prototype in operation, so that the engineer may develop knowledge and understanding of production problems.

Research-and-development technicians help to make and assemble new instruments and apparatus in close cooperation with scientists and engineers. The opportunities for self-expression and innovation are highest in this area.

EARNINGS

Salaries and wages vary according to the industry and the type of work the technician is doing. In general, starting salaries for technicians who have completed a two-year postsecondary training program range from around $20,000 to $25,000 a year. Technicians involved in apprenticeship training may receive reduced wages during the early stages of their apprenticeships. Technicians who have not completed a two-year training program receive starting salaries several hundred dollars a year less than technicians in the same industry who have completed such a program.

Most technicians who are graduates of these programs and who have advanced beyond the entry level earn salaries that range from $21,000 to $31,000 a year and average around $26,000 a year. Senior technicians receive salaries ranging from $35,000 to $55,000 a year, or more, depending on their employers and type of work performed.

Precision instrument and equipment repairers earned salaries that ranged from less than $31,730 to $73,230 or more in 2008, according to the U.S. Department of Labor.

Benefits for optics technicians depend on the employer; however, they usually include such items as health insurance, retirement or 401(k) plans, and paid vacation days.

WORK ENVIRONMENT

In some polishing and hand-figuring rooms, and in the first assembly rooms, it is sometimes necessary to provide special dust, humidity, and temperature controls. Technicians are required to wear clean, lint-free garments, and to use caps and overshoe covers. These rooms are widely used whenever the work requires the most meticulous cleanliness, since a single piece of lint might cause the loss of an entire component or assembly.

On the other hand, technicians working with large astronomical telescopes, with missile-tracking cameras on a military test range, or with instrument cameras for recording outdoor activities will have to work in a variety of conditions.

Very often, optics technicians, particularly those associated with the assembly, alignment, and testing of complete instruments, will find themselves working in the dark or at night. In very few cases is the work apt to be grimy or dangerous.

Part of the discipline of optics is scientific and technical, and another part calls for the skilled hands and eyes of the artisan. For prospective optics technicians who have an interest in and an aptitude for both of these kinds of activities, optics technology provides many opportunities to make personal contributions to the advancement and development of optical science and the optical industry.

Because optics technology is involved in creating the instruments and equipment necessary in ever-expanding fields such as medical research, space exploration, communications systems, and microcircuitry design and manufacture, optics technicians can feel some satisfaction in knowing that they are working in some of today's most exciting fields of scientific and technological research. The work that optics technicians perform directly affects the lives of most Americans.

As with all technicians in the engineering and science field, optics technicians are often called upon to perform both very challenging and very routine and repetitive work. Optics technology offers technicians a spectrum of jobs, so prospective technicians can choose those that fit their temperaments. However, almost all technicians should expect some mixture of the routine and the challenging in their jobs.

Optics technicians almost always work as part of a group effort. Often they serve as intermediaries between scientists and engineers who run projects and skilled craftsworkers who carry out much of the work.

OUTLOOK

Applications that utilize optics technology have been growing steadily in the past decade. The increasing use of fiber optics is creating new opportunities in defense and medical fields. Employment is expected to increase about as fast as the average in manufacturing as firms invest in automated machinery. Most job openings will arise from the need to replace technicians who transfer to other occupations or leave the labor force. Only a small number of job openings will be created each year because the occupation is relatively small.

Traditionally, the space program and weapons-development programs run by the military have employed large numbers of optics technicians. Employment in this field is determined by levels of government spending and is difficult to predict. Even if there are cutbacks in this spending, however, the public demand for modern complex cameras, binoculars, and telescopes and the need for advanced medical equipment should sustain employment levels for most kinds of optics technicians.

FOR MORE INFORMATION

For information on optics and career opportunities, contact
American Precision Optics Manufacturers Association
PO Box 20001
Rochester, NY 14602-0001
Email: info@apoma.org
http://www.apoma.org

For information on optics and careers in the field, visit
Exploring the Science of Light!
http://www.opticsforteens.org

For information on technician careers and optical engineering, contact
Junior Engineering Technical Society
1420 King Street, Suite 405
Alexandria, VA 22314-2750
Tel: 703-548-5387
Email: jetsinfo@jets.org
http://www.jets.org

For information on student membership, optics, and job listings, contact
Optical Society of America
2010 Massachusetts Avenue, NW
Washington, DC 20036-1012
Tel: 202-223-8130
http://www.osa.org

For information on educational training in optics, visit
Optics and Photonics Education Directory
http://www.opticseducation.org

For information on careers, educational programs, and job listings, contact
SPIE—The International Society for Optical Engineering
PO Box 10
Bellingham, WA 98227-0010
Tel: 360-676-3290
http://www.spie.org

For career advice on issues such as networking, interviewing, and job searching in the field of optics, visit the following Web site organized by the Optical Society of America:
Work in Optics
http://www.workinoptics.com

Packaging Machinery Technicians

OVERVIEW

Packaging machinery technicians work with automated machinery that packages products into bottles, cans, bags, boxes, cartons, and other containers. The machines perform various operations, such as forming, filling, closing, labeling, and marking. The systems and technologies that packaging machinery technicians work with are diverse. Depending on the job, packaging machinery technicians may work with electrical, mechanical, hydraulic, or pneumatic systems. They also may work with computerized controllers, fiber-optic transmitters, robotic units, and vision systems.

HISTORY

Packaging has been used since ancient times, when people first wrapped food in materials to protect it or devised special carriers to transport items over long distances. One of the oldest packaging materials, glass, was used by Egyptians as early as 3000 B.C. Packaging as we know it, though, has its origins in the industrial revolution. Machinery was used for mass production of items, and manufacturers needed some way to package products and protect them during transport. Packages and containers were developed that not only kept goods from damage during shipment, but also helped to increase the shelf life of perishable items.

Initially, packaging was done by hand. Workers at manufacturing plants hand-packed products into paper boxes, steel cans, glass jars, or other containers as they were produced. As manufacturing processes and methods improved, equipment and machines were developed to provide quicker and less expensive ways to package products. Automated machinery was in use by the 19th century and was used not only to package products but also to create packaging materials. The first containers produced through automated machinery were glass containers created by Michael Owens in Toledo, Ohio, in 1903.

The use of new packaging materials, such as cellophane in the 1920s and aluminum cans in the early 1960s, required updated machinery to handle the new materials and to provide faster, more efficient production. Semiautomatic machines and eventually high-speed, fully automated machines were created to handle a wide variety of products, materials, and packaging operations. Today, packaging engineers, packaging machinery technicians, and other engineering professionals work to develop new equipment and techniques that are more time-, material-, and cost-efficient. Advanced technologies, such as robotics, are allowing for the creation of increasingly sophisticated packaging machinery.

THE JOB

Packaging machinery technicians work in packaging plants of various industries or in the plants of packaging machinery manufacturers. Their jobs entail building machines, installing and setting up equipment, training operators to use the equipment, maintaining equipment, troubleshooting, and repairing machines. Many of the machines today are computer-controlled and may include robotic or vision-guided applications.

Machinery builders, also called *assemblers,* assist engineers in the development and modification of new and existing machinery designs. They build different types of packaging machinery by following engineering blueprints, wiring schematics, pneumatic diagrams, and plant layouts. Beginning with a machine frame that has been welded in another department, they assemble electrical circuitry, mechanical components, and fabricated items that they may have made themselves in the plant's machine shop. They may also be responsible for bolting on additional elements of the machine to the frame. After the machinery is assembled, they perform a test run to make sure it is performing according to specifications.

Field service technicians, also called *field service representatives*, are employed by packaging machinery manufacturers. They do most of their work at the plants where the packaging machinery is being used. In some companies, assemblers may serve as field service technicians; in others, the field service representative is a technician other than the assembler. In either case, they install new machinery at customers' plants and train in-plant machine operators and maintenance personnel on its operation and maintenance.

When a new machine is delivered, the field service technicians level it and anchor it to the plant floor. Then, following engineering drawings, wiring plans, and plant layouts, they install the system's electrical and electromechanical components. They also regulate the controls and setup for the size, thickness, and type of material to be processed and ensure the correct sequence of processing stages. After installation, the technicians test-run the machinery and make any necessary adjustments. Then they teach machine operators the proper operating and maintenance procedures for that piece of equipment. The entire installation process, which may take a week, is carefully documented. Field service representatives may also help the plant's in-house mechanics troubleshoot equipment already in operation, including modifying equipment for greater efficiency and safety.

Automated packaging machine mechanics, also called *maintenance technicians*, perform scheduled preventive maintenance as well as diagnose machinery problems and make repairs. Preventive maintenance is done on a regular basis following the manufacturer's guidelines in the service manual. During routine maintenance, technicians change filters in vacuum pumps, grease fittings, change oil in gearboxes, and replace worn bushings, chains, and belts. When machines do break down, maintenance technicians must work quickly to fix them so that production can resume as soon as possible. The technician might be responsible for all the machinery in the plant, one or more packaging lines, or a single machine. In a small plant, a single technician may be responsible for all the duties required to keep a packaging line running, while in a large plant a team of technicians may divide the duties.

REQUIREMENTS
High School
Although a high school diploma is not required, most employers who hire packaging or engineering technicians prefer employees to have one. In high school, you should take geometry and vo-tech classes such as electrical shop, machine shop, and mechanical drawing. Computer classes, including computer-aided design, are also helpful. In addition to developing mechanical and electrical abilities, you should develop communication skills through English and writing classes.

Postsecondary Training

Many employers prefer to hire technicians who have completed a two-year technical training program. Completing a machinery training program or packaging machinery program can provide you with the necessary knowledge and technical skills for this type of work. Machinery training programs are available at community colleges, trade schools, and technical institutes throughout the country, but there are only a few technical colleges specializing in packaging machinery programs. These programs award either a degree or certificate in automated packaging machinery systems.

Packaging machinery programs generally last two years and include extensive hands-on training as well as classroom study. You will learn to use simple hand tools, such as hacksaws, drill presses, lathes, mills, and grinders. Other technical courses cover sheet metal and welding work, power transmission, electrical and mechanical systems, maintenance operations, industrial safety, and hazardous materials handling.

Classes in packaging operations include bag making, loading, and closing; case loading; blister packaging; palletizing, conveying, and accumulating; and labeling and bar coding. There are also classes in form fill, seal wrap, and carton machines as well as packaging quality control and package design and testing. Courses especially critical in an industry where technology is increasingly sophisticated are PLC (programmable logic control), CAD/CAM (computer-aided design and manufacturing), fiber optics, robotics, and servo controls.

Certification or Licensing

Although employers may not require certification, it can provide a competitive advantage when seeking employment. A voluntary certification program is available for engineering technicians through the National Institute for Certification in Engineering Technologies (NICET). Certification is available at various levels and in different specialty fields. Most programs require passing a written exam and possessing a certain amount of work experience. The Institute of Packaging Professionals offers the following voluntary certifications: certified professional in training (for professionals with less than six years of experience in packaging) and certified packaging professional (for professionals with at least six years of experience in packaging).

Union membership may be a requirement for some jobs, depending on union activity at a particular company. Unions are more likely found in large-scale national and international corporations. Field service technicians are usually not unionized. Maintenance technicians and assemblers may be organized by the International Brotherhood of Teamsters or the International Association of Machinists and

Aerospace Workers. In addition, some technicians may be represented by the International Longshore and Warehouse Union.

Other Requirements

If you are interested in this field, you should have mechanical and electrical aptitudes, manual dexterity, and the ability to work under deadline pressure. In addition, you should have analytical and problem-solving skills. The ability to communicate effectively with people from varying backgrounds is especially important as packaging machinery technicians work closely with engineers, plant managers, customers, and machinery operators. You need to be able to listen to workers' problems as well as to explain things clearly. Packaging machinery technicians frequently have to provide written reports, so good writing skills are beneficial.

EXPLORING

You can test your interest in this type of work by engaging in activities that require mechanical and electrical skills, such as building a short-wave radio, taking appliances apart, and working on cars, motorcycles, and bicycles. Participating in science clubs and contests can also provide opportunities for working with electrical and mechanical equipment and building and repairing things. Taking vocational shop classes can also help you explore your interests and acquire useful skills.

Consider visiting a plant or manufacturing company to observe packaging operations and see packaging machinery technicians at work. Many plants provide school tours, and you may be able to arrange a visit through a school counselor or teacher. Reading trade publications can also familiarize you with the industry.

EMPLOYERS

Packaging machinery technicians are usually employed by companies that manufacture packaging machinery or by companies that package the products they produce. Packaging is one of the largest industries in the United States, so jobs are plentiful across the country, in small towns and large cities. Opportunities in the packaging field can be found in almost any company that produces and packages a product. Food, chemicals, cosmetics, electronics, pharmaceuticals, automotive parts, hardware, plastics, and almost any products one can think of need to be packaged before reaching the consumer market. Because of this diversity, jobs are not restricted to any product, geographic location, or plant size.

STARTING OUT

If you are enrolled in a technical program you may find job leads through your school's office of career services. Many jobs in packaging are unadvertised—you can only find out about them through contacts with professionals in the industry. You can also learn about openings from teachers, school administrators, and industry contacts acquired during training.

You can apply directly to machinery manufacturing companies or companies with manufacturing departments. Local employment offices may list job openings. Sometimes companies hire part-time or summer help in other departments, such as the warehouse or shipping. These jobs may provide an opportunity to move into other areas of the company.

ADVANCEMENT

Technicians usually begin in entry-level positions and work as part of an engineering team. They may advance from a maintenance technician to an assembler, and then move up to a supervisory position in production operations or packaging machinery. They can also become project managers and field service managers.

Workers who show an interest in their work, who learn quickly, and have good technical skills can gradually take on more responsibilities and advance to higher positions. The ability to work as part of a team and communicate well with others, plus self-motivation and the ability to work well without a lot of supervision, are all helpful traits for advancement. People who have skills as a packaging machinery technician can usually transfer those skills to engineering technician positions in other industries.

Some packaging machinery technicians pursue additional education to qualify as an engineer and move into packaging engineering, electrical engineering, mechanical engineering, or industrial engineering positions. Other technicians pursue business, economics, and finance degrees and use these credentials to obtain positions in other areas of the manufacturing process, in business development, or in areas such as importing or exporting.

EARNINGS

Earnings vary with geographical area and the employee's skill level and specific duties and job responsibilities. Other variables that may affect salary include the size of the company and the type of industry, such as the food and beverage industry or the electronics industry. Technicians who work at companies with unions generally, but not always, earn higher salaries.

In general, technicians earn approximately $20,000 a year to start and with experience can increase their salaries to approximately $33,000. Seasoned workers with two-year degrees who work for large companies may earn between $50,000 and $70,000 a year, particularly those in field service jobs or in supervisory positions.

In 2008 median hourly earnings for industrial machinery mechanics were $20.99 (or $43,670 annually), according to the U.S. Department of Labor. Hourly earning ranged from $13.63 an hour (or $28,350 annually) to $31.40 or more per hour (or $65,300 annually).

Packaging machinery technicians who are certified by the Institute of Packaging Professionals (IoPP) earn higher salaries than technicians who are not certified. According to an IoPP survey, certified packaging professionals earn between 7 percent and 10 percent more than non certified workers.

Benefits vary and depend upon company policy but generally include paid holidays, vacations, sick days, and medical and dental insurance. Some companies also offer tuition assistance programs, pension plans, profit sharing, and 401(k) plans.

WORK ENVIRONMENT

Packaging machinery technicians work in a variety of environments. They may work for a machinery manufacturer or in the manufacturing department of a plant or factory. Most plants are clean and well ventilated, although actual conditions vary based on the type of product manufactured and packaged. Certain types of industries and manufacturing methods can pose special problems. For example, plants involved in paperboard and paper manufacturing may have dust created from paper fibers. Workers in food plants may be exposed to strong smells from the food being processed, although most workers usually get accustomed to this. Pharmaceutical and electronic component manufacturers may require special conditions to ensure that the manufacturing environments are free from dirt, contamination, and static. Clean-air environments may be special rooms that are temperature- and moisture-controlled, and technicians may be required to wear special clothing or equipment when working in these rooms.

In general, most plants have no unusual hazards, although safety practices need to be followed when working on machinery and using tools. The work is generally not strenuous, although it does involve carrying small components and hand tools, and some bending and stretching.

Most packaging machinery technicians work 40 hours a week, although overtime may be required, especially during the installation of new machinery or when equipment malfunctions. Some technicians may be called in during the evening or on weekends to repair machinery that has shut down production operations. Installation and testing periods of new equipment can also be very time-intensive and stressful when problems develop. Troubleshooting, diagnosing problems, and repairing equipment may involve considerable time as well as trial-and-error testing until the correct solution is determined.

Technicians who work for machinery manufacturers may be required to travel to customers' plants to install new machinery or to service or maintain existing equipment. This may require overnight stays or travel to foreign locations.

OUTLOOK

The U.S. Department of Labor predicts that employment for packaging machinery technicians will grow more slowly than the average for all careers through 2018. However, the growth of the packaging industry, which grosses more than $100 billion a year, and a nationwide shortage of trained packaging technicians has created demand for qualified professionals. There are far more openings than there are qualified applicants.

The packaging machinery industry is expected to continue its growth in the next decade. American-made packaging machinery has earned a worldwide reputation for high quality and is known for its outstanding control systems and electronics. Continued success in global competition will remain important to the packaging machinery industry's prosperity and employment outlook.

The introduction of computers, robotics, fiber optics, and vision systems into the industry has added new skill requirements and job opportunities for packaging machinery technicians. There is already widespread application of CAD/CAM technology. The use of computers in packaging machinery will continue to increase, with computers communicating with other computers on the status of operations and providing diagnostic maintenance information and production statistics. The role of robotics, fiber optics, and electronics will also continue to expand. To be prepared for the jobs of the future, packaging machinery students should seek training in the newest technologies.

With packaging being one of the largest industries in the United States, jobs can be found across the country, in small towns and large cities, in small companies or multiplant international corporations. The jobs are not restricted to any one industry or geographical location—wherever there is industry, there is some kind of packaging going on.

FOR MORE INFORMATION

For information on certification and the packaging industry, contact
Institute of Packaging Professionals
1601 North Bond Street, Suite 101
Naperville, IL 60563-0114
Tel: 630-544-5050
Email: info@iopp.net
http://www.iopp.org

For information on certification, contact
National Institute for Certification in Engineering Technologies
1420 King Street
Alexandria, VA 22314-2750
Tel: 888-476-4238
http://www.nicet.org

For information on educational programs, contact
National Institute of Packaging, Handling, and Logistics Engineers
177 Fairsom Court
Lewisburg, PA 17837-6844
Tel: 866-464-7453
Email: niphle@dejazzd.com
http://www.niphle.org

For industry information, contact
Packaging Machinery Manufacturers Institute
4350 North Fairfax Drive, Suite 600
Arlington, VA 22203-1632
Tel: 888-275-7664
Email: pmmiwebhelp@PMMI.org
http://www.pmmi.org

Radiation Protection Technicians

QUICK FACTS

School Subjects
Mathematics
Physics

Personal Skills
Mechanical/manipulative
Technical/scientific

Work Environment
Indoors and outdoors
Primarily one location

Minimum Education Level
Associate's degree

Salary Range
$23,740 to $37,310 to
$63,260+

Certification or Licensing
Voluntary

Outlook
About as fast as the average

DOT
199

GOE
02.08.04

NOC
2263

O*NET-SOC
19-4051.00, 47-4041.00

OVERVIEW

Radiation protection technicians, also known as *nuclear technicians,* monitor radiation levels, protect workers, and decontaminate radioactive areas. They work under the supervision of nuclear scientists, engineers, or power plant managers and are trained in the applications of nuclear and radiation physics to detect, measure, and identify different kinds of nuclear radiation. They know federal regulations and permissible levels of radiation. There are approximately 6,400 radiation protection technicians employed in the United States.

HISTORY

All forms of energy have the potential to endanger life and property. This potential existed with the most primitive uses of fire, and it exists in the applications of nuclear power. Special care must be taken to prevent uncontrolled radiation in and around nuclear power plants. Skilled nuclear power plant technicians are among the workers who monitor and control radiation levels.

Around 1900, scientists discovered that certain elements give off invisible rays of energy. These elements are said to be radioactive, which means that they emit radiation. Antoine-Henri Becquerel, Marie Curie, and Pierre Curie discovered and described chemical radiation before the turn of the century. In 1910 Marie Curie isolated pure radium, the most radioactive natural element, and in 1911 she was awarded the Nobel Prize for chemistry for her work related to radiation.

Scientists eventually came to understand that radiation has existed in nature since the beginning of time, not only in specific elements on earth, such as uranium, but also in the form of cosmic rays from outer space. All parts of the earth are constantly bombarded by a certain background level of radiation, which is considered normal or tolerable.

During the 20th century, research into the nature of radiation led to many controlled applications of radioactivity, ranging from X rays to nuclear weapons. One of the most significant of these applications, which has impacted our everyday life, is the use of nuclear fuel to produce energy. Nuclear power reactors produce heat that is used to generate electricity.

Scientists are still trying to completely understand the biological effects of radiation exposure, but we know that short-term effects include nausea, hemorrhaging, and fatigue; long-range and more dangerous effects include cancer, lowered fertility, and possible birth defects. These factors have made it absolutely clear that if radiation energy is to be used for any purpose, the entire process must be controlled. Thus, appropriate methods of radiation protection and monitoring have been developed. The radiation protection technician's job is to ensure that these methods are employed accurately and consistently.

THE JOB

Radiation protection technicians protect workers, the general public, and the environment from overexposure to radiation. Many of their activities are highly technical in nature: they measure radiation and radioactivity levels in work areas and in the environment by collecting samples of air, water, soil, plants, and other materials; they record test results and inform the appropriate personnel when tests reveal deviations from acceptable levels; they help power plant workers set up equipment that automatically monitors processes within the plant and records deviations from established radiation limits; and they calibrate and maintain such equipment using hand tools.

Radiation protection technicians work efficiently with people of different technical backgrounds. They instruct operations personnel in making the necessary adjustments to correct problems such as excessive radiation levels, discharges of radionuclide materials above acceptable levels, or improper chemical levels. They also prepare reports for supervisory and regulatory agencies.

Radiation protection technicians are concerned with ionizing radiation, particularly three types known by the Greek words *alpha*, *beta*, and *gamma*. Ionization occurs when atoms split and produce charged particles. If these particles strike the cells in the body, they cause damage by upsetting well-ordered chemical processes.

In addition to understanding the nature and effects of radiation, technicians working in nuclear power plants understand the principles of nuclear power plant systems. They have a thorough knowledge of the instrumentation that is used to monitor radiation in every part of the plant and its immediate surroundings. They also play an important role in educating other workers about radiation monitoring and control.

Radiation protection technicians deal with three basic radiation concepts: time, distance from the radiation source, and shielding. When considering time, technicians know that certain radioactive materials break down into stable elements in a matter of days or even minutes. Other materials, however, continue to emit radioactive particles for thousands of years. Radiation becomes less intense in proportion to its distance from the source, so distance is an important concept in controlling radiation exposure. Shielding is used to protect people from radiation exposure. Appropriate materials with a specific thickness must be used to block emission of radioactive particles.

Because radiation generally cannot be seen, heard, or felt, radiation protection technicians use special instruments to detect and measure it and to determine the extent of radiation exposure. Technicians use devices that measure the ionizing effect of radiation on matter to determine the presence of radiation and, depending on the instrument used, the degree of radiation danger in a given situation.

Two such devices are Geiger counters and dosimeters, which measure received radiation doses. Dosimeters are often in the form of photographic badges worn by personnel and visitors. These badges are able to detect radioactivity because it shows up on photographic film. Radiation protection technicians calculate the amount of time that personnel may work safely in contaminated areas, considering maximum radiation exposure limits and the radiation level in the particular area. They also use specialized equipment to detect and analyze radiation levels and chemical imbalances.

Finally, although the radiation that is released into the environment surrounding a nuclear facility is generally far less than that released through background radiation sources, radiation protection technicians must be prepared to monitor people and environments during abnormal situations and emergencies.

Under normal working conditions, technicians monitor the workforce, the plant, and the nearby environment for radioactive contamination; test plant workers for radiation exposure, both internally and externally; train personnel in the proper use of monitoring and safety equipment; help *nuclear materials handling technicians* prepare and monitor radioactive waste shipments; perform basic radiation orientation training; take radiation contamination and control surveys, air sample surveys, and radiation level surveys; maintain and calibrate radiation detection instruments using standard samples to determine

During a training exercise, technicians check the grounds of a power plant for sources of radiation. *(David Veis, AP Photo/CTK)*

accuracy; ensure that radiation protection regulations, standards, and procedures are followed and records are kept of all regular measurements and radioactivity tests; and carry out decontamination procedures that ensure the safety of plant workers and the continued operation of the plant.

REQUIREMENTS

High School
You should have a solid background in basic high school mathematics and science. Take four years of English, at least two years of mathematics including algebra, and at least one year of physical science, preferably physics with laboratory instruction. Computer programming and applications, vocational machine shop operations, and blueprint reading will also provide you with a good foundation for further studies.

Postsecondary Training
After high school, you will need to study at a two-year technical school or community college. Several public or private technical colleges offer programs designed to prepare nuclear power plant radiation protection technicians. Other programs, called nuclear technology or nuclear materials handling technology, also provide a good foundation. You should be prepared to spend from one to two years in postsecondary technical training taking courses in chemistry, physics, laboratory procedures, and technical writing. Because the job entails

accurately recording important data and writing clear, concise technical reports, technicians need excellent writing skills.

A typical first year of study for radiation protection technicians includes introduction to nuclear technology, radiation physics, mathematics, electricity and electronics, technical communications, radiation detection and measurement, inorganic chemistry, radiation protection, blueprint reading, quality assurance/quality control, nuclear systems, computer applications, and radiation biology.

Course work in the second year includes technical writing, advanced radiation protection, applied nuclear chemistry, radiological emergencies, advanced chemistry, radiation shielding, radiation monitoring techniques, advanced radionuclide analysis, occupational safety and health, nuclear systems and safety, radioactive materials disposal and management, and industrial economics.

Students who graduate from nuclear technician programs are usually hired by nuclear power plants and other companies and institutions involved in nuclear-related activities. These employers provide a general orientation to their operations and further training specific to their procedures.

Certification or Licensing

At present, there are no special requirements for licensing or certification of nuclear power plant radiation protection technicians. Some graduates of radiation control technology programs, however, may want to become nuclear materials handling technicians. For this job, licensing may be required, but the employer usually will arrange for the special study needed to pass the licensing test.

Radiation protection professionals may become registered by completing an examination consisting of 150 multiple choice questions from the following general categories: applied radiation protection, detection and measurements, and fundamentals. This examination is administered by the National Registry of Radiation Protection Technologists. Professionals who successfully complete this examination are known as registered radiation protection technologists. Registration is not the same as licensing and does not guarantee professional ability, but it can help a technician demonstrate his or her professional competency to prospective employers.

Other Requirements

The work of a radiation protection technician is very demanding. Technicians must have confidence in their ability to measure and manage potentially dangerous radioactivity on a daily basis. Radiation protection technicians play an important teaching role in the nuclear energy–fueled power plant. They must know the control measures required for every employee and be capable of explaining the reasons for such measures. Because abnormal conditions sometimes develop in the nuclear power industry, technicians must be able to withstand the stress, work long hours without making mistakes, and participate as a cooperating member of a team of experts.

Successful technicians are usually individuals who are able to confidently accept responsibility, communicate effectively in person and on paper, and enjoy doing precise work. Their participation is vital to the successful application of nuclear technology.

Federal security clearances are required for workers in jobs that involve national security. Nuclear Regulatory Commission (NRC) clearance is required for both government and private industry employees in securing related positions. Certain projects may necessitate military clearance with or without NRC clearance. Employers usually help arrange such clearances.

EXPLORING

Professional associations can provide useful information about radiation and nuclear power. Visit the Web sites of the Nuclear Energy Institute (http://www.nei.org/howitworks) and the American Nuclear Society (http://www.aboutnuclear.org) to learn more about the field.

Ask your school counselor to help you learn more about this occupation. You also can obtain information from the occupational information centers at community and technical colleges.

Your science teacher may be able to arrange field trips and invite speakers to describe various careers. Nuclear reactor facilities are unlikely to provide tours, but they may be able to furnish literature on radiation physics and radiation control. Radiation protection technicians employed at nuclear-related facilities may be invited to speak about their chosen field.

Radiation is used for medical diagnosis and treatment in hospitals all over the country. Radiology departments of local hospitals often provide speakers for science or career classes.

In addition, a utilities company with a nuclear-fired plant may be able to offer you a tour of the visitor's center at the plant, where much interesting and valuable information about nuclear power plant operation is available. Small reactors used for experiments, usually affiliated with universities and research centers, also may give tours.

EMPLOYERS

Approximately 6,400 radiation protection technicians are employed in the United States. Radiation protection technicians are employed by government agencies, such as the Department of Energy and the

Department of Defense, as well as electric power utilities that operate nuclear plants. Other than utilities (which employ 51 percent of those in the field), technicians are employed by nuclear materials handling and processing facilities, regulatory agencies, nondestructive testing firms, radiopharmaceutical industries, nuclear waste handling facilities, nuclear service firms, and national research laboratories.

STARTING OUT

The best way to enter this career is to graduate from a radiation control technology program and make use of your school's career services office to find your first job. Another excellent way to enter the career is to join the U.S. Navy and enter its technical training program for various nuclear specialties.

Graduates of radiation control technology programs are usually interviewed and recruited while in school by representatives of companies with nuclear facilities. At that time, they may be hired with arrangements made to begin work soon after graduation. Graduates from strong programs may receive several attractive job offers.

Entry-level jobs for graduate radiation protection technicians include the position of *radiation monitor*. This position involves working in personnel monitoring, decontamination, and area monitoring and reporting. Another entry-level job is *instrument calibration technician*. These technicians test instrument reliability, maintain standard sources, and adjust and calibrate instruments. *Accelerator safety technicians* evaluate nuclear accelerator operating procedures and shielding to ensure personnel safety. *Radiobiology technicians* test the external and internal effects of radiation in plants and animals, collect data on facilities where potential human exposure to radiation exists, and recommend improvements in techniques or facilities.

Hot-cell operators conduct experimental design and performance tests involving materials of very high radioactivity. *Environmental survey technicians* gather and prepare radioactive samples from air, water, and food specimens. They may handle nonradioactive test specimens for test comparisons with government standards. *Reactor safety technicians* study personnel safety through the analysis of reactor procedures and shielding and through analysis of radioactivity tests.

ADVANCEMENT

A variety of positions are available for experienced and well-trained radiation protection technicians. *Research technicians* develop new ideas and techniques in the radiation and nuclear field. *Instrument design technicians* design and prepare specifications and tests for use

Earnings for Radiation Protection Technicians by Industry, 2008

Field	Mean Annual Earnings
Scientific research and development services	$72,190
Electric power generation, transmission, and distribution	$69,750
Colleges, universities, and professional schools	$64,410
Architectural, engineering, and related services	$54,170

Source: U.S. Department of Labor

in advanced radiation instrumentation. *Customer service specialists* work in sales, installation, modification, and maintenance of customers' radiation control equipment. *Radiochemistry technicians* prepare and analyze new and old compounds, utilizing the latest equipment and techniques. *Health physics technicians* train new radiation monitors, analyze existing procedures, and conduct tests of experimental design and radiation safety. *Soils evaluation technicians* assess soil density, radioactivity, and moisture content to determine sources of unusually high levels of radioactivity. *Radioactive waste analysts* develop waste disposal techniques, inventory stored waste, and prepare waste for disposal.

Some of the most attractive opportunities for experienced radiation protection technicians include working as radiation experts for a company or laboratory, or acting as consultants. Consultants may work for nuclear engineering or nuclear industry consulting firms or manage their own consulting businesses.

EARNINGS

The earnings of radiation protection technicians who are beginning their careers depend on the radiation safety program in which they work (nuclear power, federal or state agencies, research laboratories, medical facilities, etc.). They may begin as salaried staff or be paid hourly wages. Technicians who receive hourly wages usually work in shifts and receive premium pay for overtime.

The U.S. Department of Labor reports that annual earnings of hazardous materials removal workers (including radiation protection technicians) were $37,310 in 2008. Wages ranged from less than $23,740 to more than $63,260.

Most trained technicians earn annual starting salaries of up to $25,000 a year. After three to five years of experience, they can expect to earn as much as $33,000 a year. Consultants may earn as much as $42,000 a year. Earnings are affected by whether technicians remain in their entry-level jobs or become supervisors and whether they become registered radiation protection technologists.

Technicians usually receive benefits, such as paid holidays and vacations, insurance plans, and retirement plans. Because of the rapid changes that occur in the radiation safety industry, many employers pay for job-related study and participation in workshops, seminars, and conferences.

WORK ENVIRONMENT

Depending on the employer, work environments vary from offices and control rooms to relatively cramped and cold areas of power plants.

Of all power plant employees, radiation protection technicians are perhaps best able to evaluate and protect against the radiation hazards that are an occupational risk of this field. The safety of all plant workers depends on the quality and accuracy of their work.

Radiation protection technicians wear film badges or carry pocket monitors to measure their exposure to radiation. Like all other nuclear power plant employees, technicians wear safety clothing, and radiation-resistant clothing may be required in some areas. This type of clothing contains materials that reduce the level of radiation before it reaches the human body.

In some of the work done by radiation protection technicians, radiation shielding materials, such as lead and concrete, are used to enclose radioactive materials while the technician manipulates these materials from outside the contaminated area. These procedures are called hot-cell operations. In some areas, automatic alarm systems are used to warn of radiation hazards so that proper protection can be maintained.

OUTLOOK

There are 104 nuclear power plants licensed to operate in the United States. In an effort to offset the effects of rising costs to the public for energy obtained from traditional resources, some government officials are calling for the construction of new nuclear power plants and the relicensing of existing ones. If these plants are constructed and existing plants are relicensed, radiation protection technicians will enjoy increased employment opportunities.

However, even if the nuclear power industry experiences a decline, the employment outlook for radiation protection technicians should remain strong. Technicians are needed to support radiation safety programs in Department of Energy facilities, Department of Defense facilities, hospitals, universities, state regulatory programs, federal regulatory agencies, and many industrial activities. New technicians will be needed to replace retiring technicians or technicians who leave the field for other reasons. Increased efforts to enforce and improve safety and waste management standards may also result in new jobs for technicians. Because radiation programs have been in development for more than half a century, most of the radiation safety programs are well established and rely primarily on technicians to keep them running.

FOR MORE INFORMATION

For information on careers, publications, scholarships, and seminars, contact
American Nuclear Society
555 North Kensington Avenue
LaGrange Park, IL 60526-5535
Tel: 800-323-3044
http://www.ans.org

This professional organization promotes the practice of radiation safety. For information on the latest issues, radiation facts, and membership, contact
Health Physics Society
1313 Dolley Madison Boulevard, Suite 402
McLean, VA 22101-3926
Tel: 703-790-1745
http://www.hps.org

For information on registration, contact
National Registry of Radiation Protection Technologists
PO Box 6974
Kennewick, WA 99336-0602
http://www.nrrpt.org

This organization is dedicated to the peaceful use of nuclear technologies. Visit its Web site for career information.
Nuclear Energy Institute
1776 I Street, NW, Suite 400
Washington, DC 20006-3708
Tel: 202-739-8000
http://www.nei.org

Robotics Technicians

QUICK FACTS

School Subjects
Computer science
Mathematics

Personal Skills
Mechanical/manipulative
Technical/scientific

Work Environment
Primarily indoors
Primarily one location

Minimum Education Level
High school diploma

Salary Range
$25,000 to $46,310 to
$70,000+

Certification or Licensing
None available

Outlook
More slowly than the
average

DOT
638

GOE
N/A

NOC
2232

O*NET-SOC
17.3024.01

OVERVIEW

Robotics technicians assist robotics engineers in a wide variety of tasks relating to the design, development, production, testing, operation, repair, and maintenance of robots and robotic devices. Robotics technicians may also be referred to as *electromechanical technicians, manufacturing technicians, robot mechanics, robotics repairers, robot service technicians,* and *installation robotics technicians.*

HISTORY

Robots are devices that perform tasks ordinarily performed by humans; they seem to operate with an almost-human intelligence. The idea of robots can be traced back to the ancient Greek and Egyptian civilizations. In the 1st century A.D. Hero of Alexandria invented a machine that would automatically open the doors of a temple when the priest lit a fire in the altar. During the later periods of the Middle Ages, the Renaissance, and the 17th and 18th centuries, interest in robot-like mechanisms turned mostly to automatons, devices that imitate human and animal appearance and activity but perform no useful task.

The industrial revolution inspired the invention of many different kinds of automatic machinery. One of the most important robotics inventions occurred in 1804: Joseph-Marie Jacquard's method for controlling machinery by means of a programmed set of instructions recorded on a punched paper tape that was fed into a machine to direct its movements.

The word *robot* and the concepts associated with it were first introduced in the early 1920s. They made their appearance in a play titled

R.U.R., which stands for Rossum's Universal Robots, written by Czechoslovakian dramatist Karel Capek. The play involves human-like robotic machines created to perform manual tasks for their human masters.

During the 1950s and 1960s, advances in the fields of automation and computer science led to the development of experimental robots that could imitate a wide range of human activity, including self-regulated and self-propelled movement (either on wheels or on legs), the ability to sense and manipulate objects, and the ability to select a course of action on the basis of conditions around them.

In 1954 George Devol designed the first programmable robot in the United States. He named it the Universal Automation, which was later shortened to Unimation, which also became the name of the first robot company. Hydraulic robots, controlled by numerical control programming, were developed in the 1960s and were used initially by the automobile industry in assembly line operations. By 1973 robots were being built with electric power and electronic controls, which allowed greater flexibility and increased uses.

Robotic technology has evolved significantly in the past few decades. Early robotic equipment, often referred to as first-generation robots, were simple mechanical arms or devices that could perform precise, repetitive motions at high speeds. They contained no artificial intelligence capabilities. Second-generation robots, which came into use in the 1980s, are controlled by minicomputers and programmed by computer language. They contain sensors, such as vision systems and pressure, proximity, and tactile sensors, which provide information about the outside environment. Third-generation robots, also controlled by minicomputers and equipped with sensory devices, are currently being developed. Referred to as "smart" robots, they can work on their own without supervision by an external computer or human being.

The evolution of robots is closely tied to the study of human anatomy and movement of the human body. The early robots were modeled after arms, then wrists. Second-generation robots include features that model human hands. Third-generation robots are being developed with legs and complex joint technology. They also incorporate multisensory input controls, such as ultrasonic sensors or sensors that can "sniff" and "taste."

THE JOB

The majority of robotics technicians work within the field of computer-integrated manufacturing or programmable automation. Using computer science technology, technicians help robotics engineers design and develop robots and other automated equipment, including computer software used to program robots.

Robotics technicians assist in all phases of robotics engineering. They install, repair, and maintain finished robots. Others help design and develop new kinds of robotics equipment. Technicians who install, repair, and maintain robots and robotic equipment need knowledge of electronics, electrical circuitry, mechanics, pneumatics, hydraulics, and computer programming. They use hand and power tools, testing instruments, manuals, schematic diagrams, and blueprints.

Before installing new equipment, technicians review the work order and instructional information; verify that the intended site in the factory is correctly supplied with the necessary electrical wires, switches, circuit breakers, and other parts; position and secure the robot in place, sometimes using a crane or other large tools and equipment; and attach various cables and hoses, such as those that connect a hydraulic power unit with the robot. After making sure that the equipment is operational, technicians program the robot for specified tasks, using their knowledge of its programming language. They may write the detailed instructions that program robots or reprogram a robot when changes are needed.

Once robots are in place and functioning, they may develop problems. Technicians then test components and locate faulty parts. When the problem is found, technicians may replace or recalibrate parts. Sometimes they suggest changes in circuitry or programming, or may install different end-of-arm tools on robots to allow machines to perform new functions. They may train robotics operators in how to operate robots and related equipment and help establish in-house basic maintenance and repair programs at new installations.

Companies that only have a few robots don't always hire their own robotics technicians. Instead they use *robot field technicians* who work for a robotic manufacturer. These technicians travel to manufacturing sites and other locations where robots are used to repair and service robots and robotic equipment.

Technicians involved with the design and development of new robotic devices are sometimes referred to as *robotics design technicians*. As part of a design team, they work closely with robotics engineers. The robotics design job starts as the engineers analyze the tasks and settings to be assigned and decide what kind of robotics system will best serve the necessary functions. Technicians involved with robot assembly, sometimes referred to as *robot assemblers*, commonly specialize in one aspect of robot assembly. *Materials handling technicians* receive requests for components or materials, then locate and deliver them to the technicians doing the actual assembly or those performing tests on these materials or components. *Mechanical assembly technicians* put together components and subsystems and install them in the robot. *Electrical assembly technicians* do the same work as mechanical assembly technicians but specialize in electrical components such as circuit boards and automatic switching devices. Finally, some technicians test the finished assemblies to make sure the robot conforms to the original specifications.

Other kinds of robotics technicians include *robot operators*, who operate robots in specialized settings, and *robotics trainers*, who train other employees in the installation, use, and maintenance of robots.

REQUIREMENTS

High School

In high school, you should take as many science, math, and computer classes as possible. Recommended courses are biology, chemistry, physics, algebra, trigonometry, geometry, calculus, graphics, computer science, English, speech, composition, social studies, and drafting. In addition, take shop and vocational classes that teach blueprint and electrical schematic reading, the use of hand tools, drafting, and the basics of electricity and electronics.

Postsecondary Training

Because changes occur so rapidly within this field, it is often recommended that technicians get a broad-based education that encompasses robotics but does not focus solely on robotics. Programs that provide the widest career base are those in automated manufacturing, which includes robotics, electronics, and computer science.

Although the minimum educational requirement for a robotics technician is a high school diploma, many employers prefer to hire technicians who have received formal training beyond high school. Two-year programs are available in community colleges and technical institutes that grant an associate's degree in robotics. The armed forces also offer technical programs that result in associate's degrees in electronics, biomedical equipment repair, and computer science. The military uses robotics and other advanced equipment and offers excellent training opportunities to members of the armed forces. This training is highly regarded by many employers and can be an advantage in obtaining a civilian job in robotics.

Visit http://robotics.nasa.gov/students/robo_u.php for a list of colleges and universities that offer educational programs in robotics.

Other Requirements

Because the field of robotics is rapidly changing, you should be willing to pursue additional training on an ongoing basis during your career.

A robotics technician works on a laptop computer that controls robots being used in a military project. *(Norbert von der Groeben, The Image Works)*

After completing your formal education, you may need to take additional classes in a college or university or take advantage of training offered through employers and professional associations.

To be successful in this career, you need manual dexterity, good hand-eye coordination, and mechanical and electrical aptitude.

EXPLORING

Because robotics is a relatively new field, it is important to learn as much as possible about current trends and recent technologies. Reading books and articles in trade magazines provides an excellent way to learn about what is happening in robotics technologies and expected future trends. Trade magazines with informative articles include *Robotics Engineering, Unmanned Systems,* and *Robotics and Autonomous Systems.*

You can become a robot hobbyist and build your own robots or buy toy robots and experiment with them. Complete robot kits are available through a number of companies and range from simple, inexpensive robots to highly complex robots with advanced features and accessories. Books that give instructions and helpful hints on building robots can be found at most public libraries and bookstores. In addition, relatively inexpensive and simple toy robots are available from electronics shops, department stores, and mail order companies.

You can also participate in competitions. The International Aerial Robotics Competition (http://iarc.angel-strike.com) is sponsored by the Association for Unmanned Vehicle Systems (AUVS). This competition, which requires teams of students to build complex robots, is open to college students. The AUVS also offers several other competitions; visit http://www.auvsi.org/competitions for more information. You can also visit http://robotics.arc.nasa.gov/students/students.php for information on robotics summer camps and competitions.

Another great way to learn about robotics is to attend trade shows. Many robotics and automated machinery manufacturers exhibit their products at shows and conventions. Numerous such trade shows are held every year in different parts of the country. Information about these trade shows is available through association trade magazines and periodicals.

Other activities that foster knowledge and skills relevant to a career in robotics include membership in high school science clubs, participation in science fairs, and pursuing hobbies that involve electronics, mechanical equipment, and model building.

EMPLOYERS

Robotics technicians are employed in virtually every manufacturing industry. With the trend toward automation continuing—often via the use of robots—people trained in robotics can expect to find

Books to Read: Robot Building

Arrick, Roger. *Robot Building For Dummies*. Hoboken, N.J.: For Dummies, 2003.

Gurstelle, William. *Building Bots: Designing and Building Warrior Robots*. Chicago: Chicago Review Press, 2002.

Iovine, John. *Robots, Androids, and Animatrons: 12 Incredible Projects You Can Build*. 2d ed. New York: McGraw-Hill/TAB Electronics, 2001.

McComb, Gordon, and Myke Predko. *Robot Builder's Bonanza*. 3d ed. New York: McGraw-Hill/TAB Electronics, 2006.

McComb, Gordon. *Robot Builder's Sourcebook: Over 2,500 Sources for Robotic Parts*. New York: McGraw-Hill/TAB Electronics, 2002.

employment with almost all types of manufacturing companies in the future. States that have a large number of robotics manufacturers include California, Michigan, Illinois, Indiana, Pennsylvania, Ohio, Connecticut, and Texas.

STARTING OUT

In the past, most robotics technicians previously held positions as automotive workers, machinists, millwrights, and computer repair technicians. Companies retrained them to troubleshoot and repair robots rather than hire new workers. Although this still occurs today, there are many more opportunities for formal education and training specifically in robotics engineering; robotics manufacturers are more likely to hire graduates of robotics programs, both at the technician and engineer levels.

Graduates of two- and four-year programs may learn about available openings through their schools' career services offices. It also may be possible to learn about job openings through want ads in newspapers and trade magazines.

In many cases, it will be necessary to research companies that manufacture or use robots and apply directly to them. The organizations listed at the end of this article may offer publications with classified ads, or other job search information.

Job opportunities may be good at small, start-up companies or start-up robotics units of a large companies. Many times these employers are willing to hire inexperienced workers as apprentices or assistants.

Then, when their sales and production grow, these workers have the best chances for advancement.

Other places to search for employment include advertisements in professional magazines and newspapers and job fairs.

ADVANCEMENT

After several years on the job, robotics technicians who have demonstrated their ability to handle more responsibility may be assigned some supervisory work or, more likely, will train new technicians. Experienced technicians and engineers may teach courses at their workplace or find teaching opportunities at a local school or community college.

Other routes for advancement include becoming a sales representative for a robotics manufacturing or design firm or working as an independent contractor for companies that use or manufacture robots.

With additional training and education, such as a bachelor's degree, technicians can become eligible for positions as robotics engineers.

EARNINGS

Earnings and benefits in manufacturing companies vary widely based on the size of the company, geographic location, nature of the production process, and complexity of the robots. Robotics technicians who are graduates of a two-year robotics program earn between $25,000 and $35,000 a year. With increased training and experience, technicians can earn $70,000 or more.

The U.S. Department of Labor reports that median annual earnings of electromechanical technicians were $46,310 in 2008, and the average annual salary for mechanical engineering technicians was $48,130.

Employers offer a variety of benefits that can include the following: paid holidays, vacations, personal days, and sick leave; medical, dental, disability, and life insurance; 401(k) plans, pension and retirement plans; profit sharing; and educational assistance programs.

WORK ENVIRONMENT

Robotics technicians may work either for a company that manufactures robots or a company that uses robots. Most companies that manufacture robots are relatively clean, quiet, and comfortable environments. Technicians may work in an office or on the production floor.

Technicians who work in a company that uses robots may work in noisy, hot, and dirty surroundings. Conditions vary based on the type of industry within which one works. Automobile manufacturers use a significant number of robots, as do manufacturers of electronics components and consumer goods and the metalworking industry. Workers in a foundry work around heavy equipment and in hot and dirty environments. Workers in the electronics industry generally work in very clean and quiet environments. Some robotics personnel are required to work in clean room environments, which keep electronic components free of dirt and other contaminants. Workers in these environments wear face masks, hair coverings, and special protective clothing.

Some technicians may confront potentially hazardous conditions in the workplace. Robots, after all, are often designed and used precisely because the task they perform involves some risk to humans: handling laser beams, arc-welding equipment, radioactive substances, or hazardous chemicals. When they design, test, build, install, and repair robots, it is inevitable that some technicians will be exposed to these same risks. Plant safety procedures protect the attentive and cautious worker, but carelessness in such settings can be especially dangerous.

In general, most technicians work 40-hour workweeks, although overtime may be required for special projects or to repair equipment that is shutting down a production line. Some technicians, particularly those involved in maintenance and repairs, may work shifts that include evening, late night, or weekend work.

Field service technicians travel to manufacturing sites to repair robots. Their work may involve extensive travel and overnight stays. They may work at several sites in one day or stay at one location for an extended period for more difficult repairs.

OUTLOOK

Employment opportunities for robotics technicians are closely tied to economic conditions in the United States and in the global marketplace. Although the field is currently experiencing slow growth, the Robotics Industry Association (RIA) reports that the following industry sectors are the most promising for robotics technicians: biomedical, semiconductors, electronics, life sciences, medical devices, pharmaceutical, photonics, plastics, and rubber. Opportunities are expected to be weakest in the automotive manufacturing industry. The RIA estimates that some 184,000 robots are now working in U.S. factories, making the United States the world's second largest robotics user, next to Japan.

The use of industrial robots is expected to grow as robots become more programmable and flexible and as manufacturing processes become more automated. Growth is also expected in nontraditional applications, such as education, health care, security, and nonindustrial purposes. Employment in robotics will depend on future demand for new applications, as well as available capital to spend on research and development. Competition for technician jobs will be stiff.

FOR MORE INFORMATION

For information on competitions and student membership, contact
Association for Unmanned Vehicle Systems International
2700 South Quincy Street, Suite 400
Arlington, VA 22206-2226
Tel: 703-845-9671
Email: info@auvsi.org
http://www.auvsi.org

For career information, company profiles, training seminars, and educational resources, contact
Robotic Industries Association
900 Victors Way, Suite 140
PO Box 3724
Ann Arbor, MI 48106-5210
Tel: 734-994-6088
http://www.roboticsonline.com

Visit the following Web site for information on robotics education and summer camps and programs:
The Robotics Alliance Project
National Aeronautics and Space Administration
http://robotics.nasa.gov

For information on careers and educational programs, contact
Robotics and Automation Society
Institute of Electrical and Electronics Engineers
1828 L Street, NW, Suite 1202
Washington, DC 20036-5104
http://www.ieee-ras.org

For information on educational programs, competitions, and student membership, contact
Society of Manufacturing Engineers
One SME Drive
Dearborn, MI 48121-2408
Tel: 800-733-4763
http://www.sme.org

Semiconductor Technicians

OVERVIEW

Semiconductor technicians are highly skilled workers who test new kinds of semiconductor devices being designed for use in many kinds of modern electronic equipment. They may also test samples of devices already in production to assess production techniques. They help develop and evaluate the test equipment used to gather information about the semiconductor devices. Working under the direction provided by engineers in research laboratory settings, they assist in the design and planning for later production or help to improve production yields. There are approximately 31,600 semiconductor technicians employed in the United States.

HISTORY

Semiconductors and devices utilizing them are found in nearly every electronic product made today, from complicated weapons systems and space technology to personal computers, DVD players, cellular telephones, MP3 players, and programmable coffeemakers. The manufacturing of semiconductors and microelectronics devices requires the efforts of a variety of people, from the engineers who design them, to the technicians who process, construct, and test them.

Although the word *semiconductor* is often used to refer to microchips or integrated circuits, a semiconductor is actually the basic material of these devices. Semiconductor materials are so called because they can be switched to act with properties between that of an insulator, which does not conduct electrical current, and that of a true conductor of electrical current, such as metal.

Silicon is the most common material used as a semiconductor. Other semiconductor materials may be gallium arsenide, cadmium sulfide, and selenium sulfide. Doping, or treating, these materials with substances such as aluminum, arsenic, boron, and phosphorous gives them conducting properties. By applying these substances according to a specifically designed layout, engineers and technicians construct the tiny electronic devices—transistors, capacitors, and resistors—of an integrated circuit. A microchip no larger than a fingernail may contain many thousands of these devices.

THE JOB

There are many steps that occur in processing semiconductors into integrated circuits. The technicians involved in these processes are called *semiconductor development technicians* and *semiconductor process technicians*. They may be involved in several or many of the steps of semiconductor manufacturing, depending on where they work. Often, semiconductor technicians function as a link between the engineering staff and the production staff in the large-scale manufacturing of semiconductor products.

The making of semiconductors begins with silicon. The silicon must be extremely pure in order to be of use. The silicon used for semiconductors is heated in a furnace and formed into cylinder rods between one and six inches in diameter and three or more feet in length. These rods are smoothed and polished until they are perfectly round. They are then sliced into wafers that are between one-quarter and one-half millimeter in thickness. Then the wafers are processed, by etching, polishing, heat-treating, and lapping, to produce the desired dimensions and surface finish. After the wafers are tested, measured, and inspected for any defects, they are coated with a photosensitive substance called a photoresist.

The engineering staff and the technicians assigned to assist them prepare designs for the layout of the microchip. This work is generally done using a computer-aided design (CAD) system. The large, completed design is then miniaturized as a photomask when it is applied to the wafer. The photomask is placed over the wafer and the photoresist is developed, much like film in a camera, with ultraviolet light, so that the layout of the microchip is reproduced many times on the same wafer. This work takes place in a specially equipped laboratory, or clean room, that is kept completely free of dust and other impurities. During the miniaturization process, the tiniest speck of dust will ruin the reproduction of the layout onto the wafer.

Next, the wafer is doped with the substances that will give it the necessary conducting properties. Technicians follow the layout, like a road map, when adding these substances. The proper combinations of materials create the various components of the integrated circuit. When this process is complete, the many thousands of components in the wafer are tested by computerized equipment in a matter of seconds. Many of the integrated circuits on the wafer will not function properly, and these are marked and discarded. After testing, the wafer is cut up into its individual chips.

The chips are then packaged by placing them in a casing usually made of plastic or ceramic, which also contains metal leads for connecting the microchip into the electronic circuitry of the device for which it will be used. It is this package that is usually referred to as a chip or semiconductor.

Semiconductor process technicians are generally responsible for the fabrication and processing of the semiconductor wafer. *Semiconductor development technicians* usually assist with the basic design and development of rough sketches of a prototype chip; they may be involved in transferring the layout to the wafer and in assembling and testing the semiconductor. Both types of technicians gather and evaluate data on the semiconductor, wafer, or chip. They are responsible for ensuring that each step of the process precisely meets test specifications, and also for identifying flaws and problems in the material and design. Technicians may also assist in designing and building new test equipment, and in communicating test data and production instructions for large-scale manufacture. Technicians may also be responsible for maintaining the equipment and for training operators on its use.

REQUIREMENTS

The nature of the microelectronics industry, in which technological advances are continuous and rapid, means that some form of higher education, whether in a two-year or four-year program, is a must. An early interest in and excitement for electronics and computers is a good indicator of someone who might be interested in this career.

High School

Math and science courses, as well as classes in computers and computer science, are requirements for students wishing to enter the semiconductor and microelectronics field. Physics and chemistry will help you understand many of the processes involved in developing and fabricating semiconductors and semiconductor components. Strong communication skills are also very important.

Postsecondary Training

Technician jobs in microelectronics and semiconductor technology require at least an associate's degree in electronics or electrical engineering or technology. Students may attend a two-year program at a community college or vocational school. Students interested in a career at the engineering level should consider studying for a bachelor's degree. The trend toward greater specialization within the industry may make a bachelor's degree more desirable over an associate's degree in the future.

An electronics engineering program will include courses in electronics theory, as well as math, science, and English courses. Students can expect to study such subjects as the principle and models of semiconductor devices; physics for solid-state electronics; solid-state theory; introduction to VLSI systems; and basic courses in computer organization, electromagnetic fundamentals, digital and analog laboratories, and the design of circuits and active networks. Companies will also provide additional training on the specific equipment and software they use. Many companies also offer training programs and educational opportunities to employees to increase their skills and their responsibilities.

Courses are available at many community and junior colleges, which may be more flexible in their curriculum and better able to keep up with technological advances than vocational training schools. The latter, however, will often have programs geared specifically to the needs of the employers in their area and may have job placement programs and relationships with the different companies available as well. If you are interested in these schools, you should do some research to determine whether the training offered is thorough and that the school has a good placement record. Training institutes should also be accredited by the Accrediting Commission of Career Schools and Colleges of Technology (http://www.accsct.org).

Military service may also provide a strong background in electronics. In addition, the tuition credits available to military personnel will be helpful when continuing your education.

Certification or Licensing

Certification is not mandatory, but voluntary certification may prove useful in locating work and in increasing your pay and responsibilities. The International Society of Certified Electronics Technicians (ISCET) offers certification testing at various levels and fields of electronics. The ISCET also offers a variety of study and training material to help prepare for the certification tests.

Other Requirements

A thorough understanding of semiconductors, electronics, and the production process is necessary for semiconductor technicians. Investigative and research skills, and a basic knowledge of computers and computer programs are important for the prospective semiconductor technician. "You have to be very patient and not easily discouraged to work in this industry," says Jan Gilliam, a semiconductor technician at Advanced Micro Devices, located in Austin, Texas. "You have to really focus on the goal while paying close attention to details."

EXPLORING

You can develop your interests in computers and microelectronics while in school. Most high schools will be unable to keep up with the rapid advances in electronics technology, and you will need to read and explore on your own. Joining extracurricular clubs in computers or electronics will give you an opportunity for hands-on learning experiences.

You should also begin to seek out the higher education appropriate for your future career interests. Your high school counselor should be able to help you find a training program that will match your career goals.

EMPLOYERS

Approximately 31,600 semiconductor technicians are employed in the United States. Finding a job in the semiconductor industry may mean living in the right part of the country. Certain states, such as California, Texas, and Massachusetts, have many more opportunities than others. Some of the big names in semiconductors include Intel, Motorola, Texas Instruments, and National Semiconductor. These companies are very large and employ many technicians, but there are smaller and mid-size companies in the industry as well.

STARTING OUT

Semiconductor technician positions can be located through the career services office of a community college or vocational training school. Since an associate's degree is recommended, many of these degree programs provide students with job interviews and introductions to companies in the community that are looking for qualified workers.

Job listings in newspapers or at local employment agencies are also good places for locating job opportunities. Aspiring semiconductor technicians can also find less-skilled positions in the semiconductor industry and work hard for promotion to a technician position. Having more education and training will give you an advantage in the huge job market for semiconductors and related devices.

ADVANCEMENT

As with any manufacturing industry, the advancement possibilities available to semiconductor technicians will depend on their levels of skill, education, and experience. Technicians may advance to *senior technicians* or may find themselves in supervisory or management positions. Technicians with two-year associate's degrees may elect to continue their education. Often, their course work will be transferable to a four-year engineering program, and many times their employer may help pay for their continuing education. Semiconductor technicians may ultimately choose to enter the engineering and design phases of the field. Also, a background in semiconductor processing and development may lead to a career in sales or purchasing of semiconductor components, materials, and equipment.

EARNINGS

Semiconductor technicians earned a median hourly wage of $15.49, or $32,230 a year, in 2008, according to the U.S. Department of Labor. Ten percent of all workers earned less than $10.57 an hour ($21,980 a year), while the top paid 10 percent earned $24.23 or more an hour ($50,400 a year). Technicians earning higher salaries have more education or have worked in the industry for many years.

Benefits for semiconductor technicians depend on the employer; however, they usually include such items as health insurance, retirement or 401(k) plans, and paid vacation days.

WORK ENVIRONMENT

The work of semiconductor technicians is not physically strenuous and is usually done in an extremely clean environment. Technicians may work with hazardous chemicals, however, and proper safety precautions must be strictly followed. Because of the large demand for semiconductors and related devices, many facilities operate with two 12-hour shifts, meaning that a technician may be assigned to the night or weekend shift, or on a rotating schedule.

Because of the need for an extremely clean environment, technicians are required to wear clean-suits to keep dust, lint, and dirt out of the clean room where the production takes place.

An important component in most manufacturing processes is the speed with which products are produced. Workers may find themselves under a great deal of pressure to maintain a certain level of production volume. The ability to work well in a sometimes-stressful environment is an important quality for any prospective semiconductor technician.

OUTLOOK

The U.S. Department of Labor predicts there will be a decline in employment in the semiconductor industry through 2018. This decline is due to two main factors: higher productivity and increased imports. Many semiconductor manufacturers have installed new machinery that can produce twice as many wafers as the old machines. This increased automation has streamlined the staff of many manufacturing plants. In addition, manufacturers have begun to build plants in overseas locations where semiconductors can be made more cheaply than in the United States. In addition, imports of more affordable semiconductors from non-U.S. manufacturers is expected to rise in the coming years, which will lessen the need for semiconductor manufacturing technicians in the United States.

Despite this decline, semiconductors will be in greater demand than ever before, due to the increasing number of electronics and computers that use them. For example, the 64-bit microchip, which provide desktop computers with greater power and memory, will lead to the development of many new electronic products, especially in the medical industry. Technicians will be needed to build the components for new products, as well as to replace the many technicians who will be reaching retirement age. Jobs will go the technicians with the most education, training, and technical experience.

FOR MORE INFORMATION

For certification information, contact
International Society of Certified Electronics Technicians
3608 Pershing Avenue
Fort Worth, TX 76107-4527
Tel: 800-946-0201
Email: info@iscet.org
http://www.iscet.org

For industry information, contact
Semiconductor Equipment and Materials International
3081 Zanker Road
San Jose, CA 95134-2127
Email: semihq@semi.org
http://www.semi.org

For information on semiconductors, a glossary of terms, and industry information, contact
Semiconductor Industry Association
181 Metro Drive, Suite 450
San Jose, CA 95110-1344
Tel: 408-436-6600
Email: mailbox@sia-online.org
http://www.sia-online.org

Surveying and Mapping Technicians

OVERVIEW

Surveying and mapping technicians help determine, describe, and record geographic areas or features. They are usually the leading assistant to the *professional surveyor*, *civil engineer*, and *mapmaker*. They operate modern surveying and mapping instruments and may participate in other operations. Technicians must have a basic knowledge of the current practices and legal implications of surveys to establish and record property size, shape, topography, and boundaries. They often supervise other assistants during routine surveying conducted within the bounds established by a professional surveyor. There are approximately 77,000 surveying and mapping technicians working in the United States.

HISTORY

Since ancient times, people have needed to define their property boundaries. Marking established areas of individual or group ownership was a basis for the development of early civilizations. Landholding became important in ancient Egypt, and with the development of hieroglyphics, people were able to keep a record of their holdings. Eventually, nations found it necessary not only to mark property boundaries but also to record principal routes of commerce and transportation. For example, records of the Babylonians tell of their canals and irrigation ditches. The Romans surveyed and mapped their empire's principal roads. In the early days of colonial exploration, surveyors and their technical helpers were among the first and most-needed workers. They established new land ownership by surveying and filing claims. Since then, precise and accurate geographical measurements have been needed to determine the location of a highway, the site of a building, the right-of-way for drainage ditches, telephone, and power lines, and for the charting of unexplored land, bodies of water, and underground mines.

Early surveying processes required at least two people. A technical scientist served as the leader, or professional surveyor. This scientist was assisted by helpers to make measurements with chains, tapes, and wheel rotations, where each rotation accounted for a known length of distance. The helpers held rods marked for location purposes and placed other markers to define important points.

As measuring instruments have become more complex, the speed, scope, and accuracy of surveying have improved. Developments in surveying and mapping technology have made it much easier to plan and construct highway systems and structures of all kinds. For roadway route selection and design, technicians increasingly use photogrammetry, which uses satellites, aerial cameras, and light-imaging detection and ranging technology to compile data about the earth's surface. Route data obtained by photogrammetry may then be processed through computers to calculate land acquisition, grading, and construction costs. Photogrammetry is faster and far more accurate than former methods. New electronic distance-measuring devices have brought surveying to a higher level of precision. Technicians can measure distance more quickly, accurately, and economically than was possible with tapes, rods, and chains.

In addition to photogrammetry, the use of computers in data processing has extended surveying and mapping careers past the earth's surface. Technicians now help to make detailed maps of ocean floors and the moon. Every rocket fired from the Kennedy Space Center is tracked electronically to determine if it is on course through the use of maps made by surveyors. The technological complexity of such undertakings allows surveyors to delegate more tasks than ever to technicians.

THE JOB

As essential assistants to civil engineers, surveyors, and mapmakers, surveying and mapping technicians are usually the first to be involved in any job that requires precise plotting. This includes highways, airports, housing developments, mines, dams, bridges, and buildings of all kinds.

The surveying and mapping technician is a key worker in field parties and major surveying projects and is often assigned the position of chief instrument worker under the surveyor's supervision.

Technicians use a variety of surveying instruments, including the theodolite, transit, level, and other electronic equipment, to measure distances or locate a position. Technicians may be *rod workers,* using level rods or range poles to make elevation and distance measurements. They may also be *chain workers,* measuring shorter distances using a surveying chain or a metal tape. During the survey, it is important to accurately record all readings and keep orderly field notes to check for accuracy.

Surveying and mapping technicians may specialize if they join a firm that focuses on one or more particular types of surveying. In a firm that specializes in land surveying, technicians are highly skilled in technical measuring and tasks related to establishing township, property, and other tract-of-land boundary lines. They help the professional surveyor with maps, notes, and title deeds. They help survey the land, check the accuracy of existing records, and prepare legal documents such as deeds and leases.

Similarly, technicians who work for highway, pipeline, railway, or power line surveying firms help to establish grades, lines, and other points of reference for construction projects. This survey information provides the exact locations for engineering design and construction work.

Technicians who work for geodetic surveyors help take measurements of large masses of land, sea, or space. These measurements must take into account the curvature of the earth and its geophysical characteristics. Their findings set major points of reference for smaller land surveys, determining national boundaries, and preparing maps.

Technicians may also specialize in hydrographic surveying, measuring harbors, rivers, and other bodies of water. These surveys are needed to design navigation systems, prepare nautical maps and charts, establish property boundaries, and plan for breakwaters, levees, dams, locks, piers, and bridges.

Mining surveying technicians are usually on the geological staffs of either mining companies or exploration companies. In recent years, costly new surveying instruments have changed the way they do their jobs. Using highly technical machinery, technicians can map underground geology, take samples, locate diamond drill holes, log drill cores, and map geological data derived from boreholes. They also map data on mine plans and diagrams and help the geologist determine ore reserves. In the search for new mines, technicians operate delicate instruments to obtain data on variations in earth's magnetic field, its conductivity, and gravity. They use their data to map the boundaries of areas for potential further exploration.

Surveying and mapping technicians may find topographical surveys to be interesting and challenging work. These surveys determine the contours of the land and indicate such features as mountains, lakes, rivers, forests, roads, farms, buildings, and other distinguishable landmarks. In topographical surveying, technicians help take aerial or land photographs with photogrammetric equipment installed in an airplane or ground station that can take pictures of large areas. This method is widely used to measure farmland planted with certain crops and to verify crop average allotments under government production planning quotas.

A large number of survey technicians are employed in construction work. Technicians are needed from start to finish on any job. They check the construction of a structure for size, height, depth, level, and form specifications. They also use measurements to locate the critical construction points as specified by design plans, such as corners of buildings, foundation points, center points for columns, walls, and other features, floor or ceiling levels, and other features that require precise measurements and location.

Technological advances such as the Global Positioning System (GPS) and Geographic Information Systems (GIS) have revolutionized surveying and mapping work. Using these systems, surveying teams can track points on the earth with radio signals transmitted from satellites and store this information in computer databases.

REQUIREMENTS
High School
If you are interested in becoming a surveying and mapping technician, take mathematics courses, such as algebra, geometry, and trigonometry, as well as mechanical drawing in high school. Physics, chemistry, and biology are other valuable classes that will help you gain laboratory experience. Reading, writing, and comprehension skills as well as knowledge of computers are also vital in surveying and mapping, so English and computer science courses are also highly recommended.

Postsecondary Training
Though not required to enter the field, graduates of accredited postsecondary training programs for surveying, photogrammetry, and mapping are in the best position to become surveying and mapping technicians. Postsecondary training is available from institutional programs and correspondence schools. These demanding technical programs generally last two years with a possible field study in the summer. First-year courses include English, composition, drafting, applied mathematics, surveying and measurements, construction materials and methods, applied physics, statistics, and computer applications. Second-year courses cover subjects such as technical physics, advanced surveying, photogrammetry and mapping, soils and founda-

A surveying technician surveys land near a highway. *(Bob Daemmrich, The Image Works)*

tions, technical reporting, legal issues, and transportation and environmental engineering. Contact the American Congress on Surveying and Mapping (ACSM) for a list of accredited programs (see the end of this article for contact information).

With additional experience and study, technicians can specialize in geodesy, topography, hydrography, or photogrammetry. Many graduates of two-year programs later pursue a bachelor's degree in surveying, engineering, or geomatics.

Certification or Licensing

Unlike professional land surveyors, there are no certification or licensing requirements for becoming a surveying and mapping technician. However, technicians who seek government employment must pass a civil service examination.

Many employers prefer certified technicians for promotions into higher positions with more responsibility. The National Society of Professional Surveyors offers the voluntary certified survey technician designation at four levels. With each level, the technician must have more experience and pass progressively challenging examinations. If the technician hopes one day to work as a surveyor, he or she must be specially certified to work in his or her state. The American Society for Photogrammetry and Remote Sensing also offers voluntary certification programs for technicians.

Other Requirements

To be a successful surveying and mapping technician, you must be patient, orderly, systematic, accurate, and objective in your work. You must be willing to work cooperatively and have the ability to think and plan ahead. Because of the increasing technical nature of their work, you must have computer skills to be able to use highly complex equipment such as GPS and GIS technology.

EXPLORING

One of the best opportunities for experience is to work part time or during your summer vacation for a construction firm or a company involved in survey work. Even if the job does not involve direct contact with survey crews, you may be able to observe their work and converse with them to discover more about their daily activities. Another possibility is to work for a government agency overseeing land use. The Bureau of Land Management, for example, has employment opportunities for students who qualify, as well as many volunteer positions. The Forest Service also offers temporary positions for students.

EMPLOYERS

There are approximately 77,000 surveying and mapping technicians working in the United States. About 70 percent of technicians find work with engineering or architectural service firms. The federal government also employs a number of technicians to work for the U.S. Geological Survey, the Bureau of Land Management, the National Oceanic and Atmospheric Administration, the National Geospatial-Intelligence Agency, and the Forest Service. State and local governments also hire surveying and mapping technicians to work for highway departments and urban planning agencies. Construction firms and oil, gas, and mining companies also hire technicians.

STARTING OUT

If you plan to enter surveying straight from high school, you may first work as an apprentice. Through on-the-job training and some classroom work, apprentices build up their skills and knowledge of the trade to eventually become surveying and mapping technicians.

If you plan to attend a technical institute or four-year college, visit your school's career services office for help in arranging examinations or interviews. Employers of surveying technicians often send recruiters to schools before graduation and arrange to employ promising graduates. Some community or technical colleges have work-study programs that provide cooperative part-time or summer work for pay. Employers involved with these programs often hire students full time after graduation.

Finally, many cities have employment agencies that specialize in placing technical workers in positions in surveying, mapping, construction, mining, and related fields. Check your local newspaper, telephone book, or surf the Web to see if your town offers these services.

ADVANCEMENT

Possibilities for advancement are linked to levels of formal education and experience. As technicians gain experience and technical knowledge, they can advance to positions of greater responsibility and eventually work as chief surveyor. To advance into this position, technicians will most likely need a two- or four-year degree in surveying and many years of experience. Also, all 50 states require surveyors to be licensed, requiring varying amounts of experience, education, and examinations.

Regardless of the level of advancement, all surveying and mapping technicians must continue studying to keep up with the technological developments in their field. Technological advances in computers, lasers, and microcomputers will continue to change job requirements. Studying to keep up with changes combined with progressive experience gained on the job will increase the technician's opportunity for advancement.

EARNINGS

According to the U.S. Department of Labor, the 2008 median hourly salary for all surveying and mapping technicians, regardless of the industry, was $16.88 (amounting to $35,120 for full-time work). The lowest paid 10 percent earned less than $10.42 ($21,680 for full-time work), and the highest paid 10 percent earned more than $27.90 an hour (or $58,030 annually for full-time work). Technicians working for the public sector in federal, state, and local governments generally earn more per hour than those working in the private sector for engineering and architectural services. In 2008 surveying and mapping technicians working for the federal government made a mean salary of $46,770 per year.

Benefits include paid vacation; health; disability and life insurance; and retirement or pension plans.

WORK ENVIRONMENT

Surveying and mapping technicians usually work about 40 hours a week except when overtime is necessary. The peak work period for many kinds of surveying work is during the summer months when weather conditions are most favorable. However, surveying crews are exposed to all types of weather conditions.

Some survey projects involve certain hazards depending upon the region and the climate as well as local plant and animal life. Field survey crews may encounter snakes and poison ivy. They are subject to heat exhaustion, sunburn, and frostbite. Some projects, particularly those being conducted near construction projects or busy highways, impose dangers of injury from cars and flying debris. Unless survey technicians are employed for office assignments, their work location changes from survey to survey. Some assignments may require technicians to be away from home for varying periods of time.

While on the job, technicians who supervise other workers must take special care to observe good safety practices. Construction and mining workplaces usually require hard hats, special clothing, and protective shoes.

OUTLOOK

Employment for surveying and mapping technicians is expected to grow faster than the average for all occupations through 2008, according to the U.S. Department of Labor. New technologies—such as GPS, GIS, and remote sensing—have increased the accuracy and productivity of professionals in the field but may reduce employment growth slightly in the short term.

One factor that may increase the demand for surveying services, and therefore surveying technicians, is growth in urban and suburban areas. New streets, homes, shopping centers, schools, and gas and water lines will require property and boundary line surveys. Other factors are the continuing state and federal highway improvement programs and the increasing number of urban redevelopment programs. The expansion of industrial and business firms and the relocation of some firms to large undeveloped areas are also expected to create a need for surveying services.

The need to replace workers who have either retired or transferred to other occupations will also provide opportunities. In general, technicians with more education and skill training will have more job options.

FOR MORE INFORMATION

For more information on accredited surveying programs, contact
Accreditation Board for Engineering and Technology
111 Market Place, Suite 1050
Baltimore, MD 21202-4012

Tel: 410-347-7700
http://www.abet.org

For information on careers and scholarships, contact
American Congress on Surveying and Mapping
Six Montgomery Village Avenue, Suite 403
Gaithersburg, MD 20879-3546
Tel: 240-632-9716
http://www.acsm.net

For information on certification, contact
American Society for Photogrammetry and Remote Sensing
5410 Grosvenor Lane, Suite 210
Bethesda, MD 20814-2160
Tel: 301-493-0290
Email: asprs@asprs.org
http://www.asprs.org

For information about the Bureau of Land Management and its responsibilities, visit its Web site.
Bureau of Land Management
Office of Public Affairs
1849 C Street, Room 406-LS
Washington, DC 20240-0001
Tel: 202-452-5125
http://www.blm.gov

For more information on Geographic Information Systems (GIS), visit
GIS.com
http://www.gis.com

For information on certification, contact
National Society of Professional Surveyors
Six Montgomery Village Avenue, Suite 403
Gaithersburg, MD 20879-3557
Tel: 240-632-9716
http://www.nspsmo.org

Welding Technicians

QUICK FACTS

School Subjects
Physics
Technical/shop

Personal Skills
Helping/teaching
Technical/scientific

Work Environment
Indoors and outdoors
Primarily multiple locations

Minimum Education Level
Some postsecondary training

Salary Range
$21,780 to $31,610 to
$49,760+

Certification or Licensing
Recommended

Outlook
More slowly than the
average

DOT
011

GOE
08.02.01, 08.03.03

NOC
7265

O*NET-SOC
51-4122.02

OVERVIEW

Welding technicians are the link between the welder and the engineer and work to improve a wide variety of welding processes. As part of their duties, they may supervise, inspect, and find applications for the welding processes. Some technicians work in research facilities, where they help engineers test and evaluate newly developed welding equipment, metals, and alloys. When new equipment is being developed or old equipment improved, they conduct experiments on it, evaluate the data, and then make recommendations to engineers. Other welding technicians, who work in the field, inspect welded joints and conduct tests to ensure that welds meet company standards, national code requirements, and customer job specifications. These technicians record the results, prepare and submit reports to welding engineers, and conduct welding personnel certification tests according to national code requirements.

HISTORY

The origins of modern welding reach back thousands of years. Archaeological evidence suggests that primitive forms of welding were known even in prehistoric times. Ancient Egyptians practiced a form of welding similar to our gas welding in which they used a blowpipe and a flame from burning alcohol to heat the metal surfaces to be welded.

During the 19th century, new methods for joining two pieces of metal were developed, and existing methods were refined. Resistance welding was developed in 1857. In this method, the metal parts to be joined are pressed together, and a surge of electrical current is sent through the metal at the point of contact. The combination of pressure and heat formed by electrical resistance results in the formation of a solid welded nugget that holds the pieces of metal together. This method was not perfected until 1886 because of the lack of sufficient electrical power.

Thermite welding, which fuses two pieces of metal by means of thermite (a mixture of aluminum and iron oxide), was first used in 1898. Arc welding, a process of fusing metal by means of heat generated from an electrical arc, was developed experimentally in 1881 and was first used commercially in 1889.

Gas welding uses the heat of burning gas, such as a mixture of acetylene and oxygen. Although oxygen was identified in 1774 and acetylene in 1836, the effect of joining the two gases was not discovered until 1895, when improved methods of commercial production of acetylene and oxygen were developed. The year 1903 marked the beginning of the commercial use of the oxyacetylene process in welding and cutting.

During the 20th century, these methods were further improved, and dozens of new methods were developed. Two other methods now commonly used are brazing and induction welding. In brazing, a filler metal is heated along with the metal surfaces and flows into a specially prepared joint. Induction welding uses an induction coil that generates heat and is very efficient for certain shapes such as small-diameter, thin-walled steel tubing.

Automated welding, in which a robot or machine completes a welding task while being monitored by a welding technician or machine operator, is becoming an increasingly popular production method.

THE JOB

Welding technicians fill positions as supervisors, inspectors, experimental technicians, sales technicians, assistants to welding engineers, and welding analysts and estimators.

Some beginning welding technicians are employed as *welding operators*. They perform manual, automatic, or semiautomatic welding jobs. They set up work, read blueprints and welding-control symbols, and follow specifications set up for a welded product.

As *welding inspectors*, welding technicians judge the quality of incoming materials, such as electrodes, and of welding work being done. They accept or reject pieces of work according to required standards set forth in codes and specifications. A welding inspector must be able to read blueprints, interpret requirements, and have a knowledge of testing equipment and methods.

Closely related to this work is that of the *welding qualification technician*. This person keeps records of certified welders and supervises tests for the qualification of welding operators.

Other welding technicians work as *welding process-control technicians*. These technicians set up the procedures for welders to follow in various production jobs. They specify welding techniques, types of filler wire to be used, ranges for welding electrodes, and time estimates. Welding technicians also provide instructions concerning welding symbols on blueprints, use of jigs and fixtures, and inspection of products.

Equipment maintenance and sales technicians work at welding supply houses. They set up equipment sold by their company, train welding operators to use it, and troubleshoot for customers.

Welding technicians may also work as *technical writers*. In this position, they work closely with professional staff members to prepare reports and develop articles for technical or professional publications. Welding technicians may also work for in-house publications or trade magazines.

After more years of experience, welding technicians may be employed as welding analysts and estimators, welding engineering assistants, or welding equipment or product salespeople. *Welding analysts and estimators* analyze all the factors involved in a job, such as labor, material, and overhead, to determine what it will cost. *Welding engineering assistants* test welded metal parts, analyze design differences for a variety of welded structures, and determine the effects of welding on a variety of metals. Some senior welding technicians may eventually advance in their companies to positions as welding supervisors, welding instructors, and welding production managers.

REQUIREMENTS

High School

To prepare for this career, you should have a good background in English, mathematics, physics, and chemistry. Courses that teach composition and communication skills are particularly important since you will need to communicate effectively with coworkers and managers. Shop courses also will prove helpful.

Postsecondary Training

Most prospective welding technicians should plan to complete a two-year associate's degree program. The U.S. Armed Forces also provide a welding technician training program.

Students pursuing a concentration in welding technology should take comprehensive courses in welding practice or theory. They also

A welding student uses welding equipment during a class. *(Jeff Greenberg, The Image Works)*

need at least one course in applied physics—covering mechanics, heat, light, elementary electricity, materials, and metallurgy—to understand metals common in industry; basic metal production and fabrication techniques; and the structures, physical and chemical properties, and uses of metals.

Welding technicians should understand lattice structure, alloy systems, mechanical tests, and characteristics of strength, elasticity, ductility, malleability, and heat treatment. Elementary chemistry, which relates to metallurgy, is usually covered in metallurgical class and laboratory study.

Another area of training helpful to the welding technician is a course in metal shaping, forming, and machine-shop practice. Knowledge of drilling, tapping, reaming, shaping, and lathe and mill operation is useful. In addition, welding technicians should have some training in electronics. They may be called upon to read an electrical wiring diagram for a particular piece of equipment or to check the voltage on a machine. Courses in nondestructive testing also are helpful for the prospective welding technician.

Certification or Licensing

Welding technicians may qualify for certification as engineering technicians. In addition, they may be certified under any of the many certification programs conducted for welders; however, certification is usually not required for technicians who do not perform actual production welding.

Other Requirements

You should enjoy working with your hands and doing research. You must be able to use drawing instruments and gauges, perform laboratory tests, and supervise and control machinery and test equipment. You will also be required to collect data and assemble it into written reports. Because welding technicians work with management as well as with production personnel, you must have a sense of responsibility and the ability to get along with people.

EXPLORING

To observe welders or welding technicians at work, ask your teacher to arrange field trips to manufacturing companies that use various welding processes. This will give you an overall view of working conditions and the type of work performed.

EMPLOYERS

Welding technicians can be found in practically any industry: aircraft, appliances, armaments, automobiles, food processing plants, nuclear energy, radio, railroads, shipbuilding, structural engineering, and television.

STARTING OUT

Graduates of accredited engineering technology programs seldom have problems finding employment. Employers usually keep in close contact with these schools and often hire able students before graduation. Most graduates of two-year welding technician programs enter industry as welding operators or as assistants to welding engineers or welding production managers. This experience forms the foundation for future problem solving and job growth, allowing the graduate technician to apply both practice and theory.

ADVANCEMENT

With experience, welding technicians become eligible for higher paying jobs. Those who advance the quickest have displayed a sense of personal initiative, especially in attending courses, seminars, and technical meetings that help broaden their knowledge and prepare them for more responsible positions.

With higher paying jobs come greater responsibilities. Some welding technicians, for instance, become *welding supervisors* and take on the responsibility of assigning jobs to workers and showing them how the tasks should be performed. They must supervise job performance and ensure that operations are performed correctly and economically. Other technicians become *welding instructors*, teaching welding theory, techniques, and related processes. Finally, some technicians advance to the position of *welding production manager*, responsible for all aspects of welding production: equipment, materials, process control, inspection, and cost control.

EARNINGS

Salaries for welding technicians vary according to the individual's function and level of education as well as the geographic location of the business. According to the U.S. Department of Labor, the median salary for welding operators and tenders (which includes welding technicians) was $31,610 in 2008. Those starting out earned approximately $21,780; however, salaries increase with experience. The highest paid technicians earned more than $49,760 a year.

Benefits for full-time workers include vacation and sick time, health, and sometimes dental, insurance, and pension or 401(k) plans. Self-employed welding technicians must provide their own benefits.

WORK ENVIRONMENT

Welding technicians are employed by a variety of industries, ranging from aircraft manufacturers to heavy-equipment plants. Working conditions vary from performing tests in clean, well-lighted research and testing laboratories to laying pipeline in the extreme heat of the desert or the cold of Alaska.

In both training and responsibility, welding technicians occupy a position between the professionally trained scientist or engineer and the skilled trade worker. Although no position carries with it the promise of complete job satisfaction, many welding technicians have found that this career offers them status and security, steady employment, and the opportunity to travel.

OUTLOOK

The U.S. Department of Labor predicts the employment of welders and welding technicians will grow more slowly than the average for all careers through 2018. Despite this prediction, there should continue to be excellent opportunities in the field. The diversity of industries in which welding technicians work helps cushion them against threats to employment caused by economic downturns for a particular industry. If economic conditions, and hence employment opportunities, become unfavorable in one industry, there remain others that require the welding technician's training and experience. Opportunities are expected to increase in the manufacturing, construction, and utilities industries.

There is an increasing variety of jobs open to welding technicians in industry. This is due to the great number of new inventions and technical processes that use an even wider variety of metals, alloys, and nonmetallic materials that can be joined by welding processes.

Most welding technicians work in industrial production settings; therefore, the actual number of welding technicians employed will be influenced by economic conditions.

FOR MORE INFORMATION

For information on welding careers, scholarships, and a free DVD and career brochure, contact
American Welding Society
550 NW LeJeune Road
Miami, FL 33126-5649
Tel: 800-443-9353
Email: info@aws.org
http://www.aws.org and http://awssection.org/index.php/forms/
  career_guide

Index

Entries and page numbers in **bold** indicate major treatment of a topic.